MW01506044

SOLO

For Nina & Koosje

EMMA DE THOUARS

SOLO

Embrace the Pleasure of Cooking for Yourself

Robert ROSE

CONTENTS

FORE

WORD

Almost every time I ask people if they like to cook, I get vague, apologetic answers that always boil down to the same thing: "Yes, I like cooking" followed by a long summary of why they almost never do it. I often hear "only when I have time" or "only if I'm cooking for friends." People in relationships do cook when their partners are home, but if they have an evening to themselves, they end up getting takeout or just grabbing a bag of chips. People who live alone often cook too much food and then are compelled to eat the same thing for days on end. I want to change that with this book.

You deserve the best of the best, even when you're eating alone. Don't worry — I won't tell you to spend hours in the kitchen because you're worth it, or that cooking for yourself is the ultimate form of self-care. While both of these things are true, let's be realistic: Most evenings, after a busy day, you have to decide what you're going to eat, get groceries, cook a meal and then do the dishes on top of it. That's exhausting. You want to be able to fall back on a few easy recipes that don't require much thought and to have an intelligently stocked fridge where you can find the perfect leftovers.

Let me help you. After all, I am an experienced expert in eating alone — I have not had a relationship or housemates in years — and most evenings I cook for myself and no one else because I love it. I'm happiest when I'm puttering around at home and spending the evening on the couch with a book, especially if I've had something tasty to eat beforehand. I've learned how to cook in small quantities over the years and how to prep meal components throughout the week, so I can quickly assemble dinner out of a few premade things. In short, I am highly skilled in the culinary management of a one-person household.

In this book, I've compiled my favorite tips and recipes for you, so that you can become just as much of an expert as me — or at least not resort to a microwavable dinner every night. Cooking for one isn't complicated; you just need to think a little differently.

Even though the number of single-person households is growing fast, the world hasn't caught on just yet. Grocery store packaging is too much for one person and most cookbooks contain recipes that serve four people. Sure, you can divide those recipes by four, but then you'll still have three-quarters of a cabbage left, for example. Cooking for yourself requires a little more planning and self-awareness, but once you get the hang of it, it's really, really fun. You can do it! I promise.

Love, Emma

SINGLE-PEOPLE

"I Throw Too Much Away"

The way food is packaged in the grocery store is often intended for two people or more. Smaller packages, if they're available at all, are super expensive. You can eat cabbage or cauliflower for days if you cook one, but usually you'll have had enough of it after day two. Herbs wilt after one week and it can be difficult to cook pasta for one. This means quite a lot of food ends up in the garbage, which is a waste.

Throwing less away means getting good at fridge management, a term that means different things for different people. My life is very predictable and I almost always eat at home. So, for me, shopping once a week works well. However, you might be more spontaneous and regularly accept last-minute dinner invitations. Doing smaller shops a few times a week might work better for you. It's about knowing what's in your fridge and how to use it creatively.

"I Don't Want to Eat the Same Thing All Week"

For many people, the best way to avoid waste is to make a meal for four anyway and then eat the same thing for days on end. This is my biggest nightmare. If you want to do meal prep all day Sunday so you can take the same meal out of the fridge every evening, be my guest, but I never eat the same thing two days in a row. Okay, sometimes leftovers for lunch, but I want something else for dinner.

I get around this by having some components of my last meal show up a different way in my next meal. For example, the fried spinach with çılbır (see page 105) is also very tasty the next day on a grilled sandwich or as part of a little plate (see page 62) with some baby potatoes, canned sardines and a dollop of crème fraîche.

PROBLEMS...

...AND HOW I WILL HELP YOU WITH THEM

"I Have So Little Space"

Unless you're fortunate enough to have a big place, you're probably making do with a small fridge and freezer. Batch freezing is unlikely to be a reality for you. So, in this book, we won't be freezing anything. The only kitchen tools you'll need are a sharp knife, a zester and an immersion blender.

"I Don't Feel Like It"

Getting motivated to cook for one is probably the hardest thing to get past. Many people think it's a waste to be standing in the kitchen for half an hour and then eating alone on the couch in five minutes.

Do you break into a sweat when a recipe tells you to "blanch the peas" or have no idea how to toast nuts? Cooking is not very relaxing if you're not confident. The more you cook, the more fun it may become for you. (Or maybe not.) Just as with exercise or reading, you do have to force yourself a little at the beginning for it to become a habit. Once it's a habit, it will feel like it takes less effort. Try cooking for yourself once or twice a week for one month (even if it's the same meals). If you still don't enjoy it after a month, you can stop and just make the easiest recipes from this book.

Most days you want to eat a tasty and nutritious meal after work, even though you have no interest in cooking. I feel the same way. There are plenty of days I look at my meal plan and almost cry: Why did I think it was a good idea to make cabbage rolls on Monday night? On those evenings, I often fall back on a rice bowl with vegan tuna (see page 82) or labneh with roasted cauliflower (see page 112). I can now cook these meals on autopilot. I hope some of the recipes in this book become so familiar to you that you can make them without thinking about it. Check out page 34 for some of my ultimate fallbacks — these are so easy I might be embarrassed to even call them recipes.

GUIDE
FOR
A

... ONE-PERSON HOUSEHOLD

Fridge Management for One

Many food issues faced by people living alone can be solved with some planning and fridge management. It doesn't need to be complicated. In the following pages, I've outlined some of my top tips. These will help you to grocery shop and use leftovers in a smart way and they explain how to make sure you're cooking an appropriate amount for one.

Planning

Don't panic — I'm not going to tell you that you have to make a rigid schedule for eating meals on a specific day or to do your shopping homework. (Although I admit, I do that sometimes, because I find it very stressful to think of what to eat once I get to the end of the day.)

The most important thing is to be honest with yourself about your cooking and eating habits. Do you eat at home often? Do you usually cook for yourself, or do you have people over for dinner regularly? Do you eat out a lot? If you made a weekly meal plan, would you be able to stick to it? Is lunch provided at work or do you pack one? Or, do you work from home with an ability to heat something up quickly from the fridge? Are you the type to go shopping without a list, getting inspired by nice ingredients and whipping things up easily? Or perhaps you don't know what to do with the ingredients in your fridge without a specific recipe? No matter what your personality, a plan can help. Here are some examples.

1. The Improviser

You're not interested in figuring out what to eat a few days from now. You may end up wanting something different or abandon the whole plan and spontaneously meet up with someone for food. You never know what life will bring, so it is for you to shop every day or every few days.

Your Plan

Make a list on your phone of a few of your favorite dishes and the ingredients you need to make them. Make sure all the ingredients can be bought in your neighborhood or on the way home. This will allow you to fall back on something tasty at the last minute without having to set your entire week in stone. You will probably end up with food left over, but fortunately I've created a leftovers guide on page 19 that will explain what to do with them to make things easier for yourself.

Keep some shelf-stable items in your pantry for when you don't feel like going to the store. A can of peeled tomatoes for a quick pasta sauce, beans or corn (canned, of course) are three great examples.

2. The Control Freak

You know what you'll be cooking every evening of every week and you rarely deviate from the schedule. You always have the ingredients on hand for the recipes you'll be cooking, which means you don't have to think when the time comes. You don't like surprises.

Your Plan

I'll use myself as an example here. Every week, I make a meal plan including breakfast, lunch and dinner for almost every day. (I usually plan out dinners for five of the seven days. I used to do every day, but I found I needed a bit of flexibility.) The only times I plan all my meals is when I'm testing recipes or want to eat certain leftovers for lunch or go wild on the weekends. I also make a list of any snack foods or snack ingredients I may need, such as bananas or dried chickpeas to make hummus. I use this plan to write my shopping list.

I shop for groceries on Saturdays, going to different stores: the market, the Asian grocery store, the wholesaler and/or Middle Eastern supermarket. My preference is to go grocery shopping every other week, generally enough for two weeks. This means I can buy a greater variety of vegetables and have a more varied diet than if I were to shop every week. I make my next meal plan based on things I still have at home and replenish some perishable items, such as yogurt or fresh herbs.

3. Something in Between

You don't mind making a weekly shopping list. You might even enjoy going to the supermarket and the nice delicatessen. Or, maybe you don't. Sometimes you cook from a recipe, but you can also improvise using what's in the fridge.

Your Plan

Every week, write down a few recipes that you'd like to make, but don't assign them to a day just yet. Get the ingredients you need for those recipes as well as any additional favorites during your weekly shop. Fall back on cooking from a recipe on days when you aren't inspired, and improvise with your staples on other days.

4. "Too Busy to Shop"

This description may overlap with all the other descriptions on this list. You lead a full life and there just isn't time to shop regularly. Or, supermarkets at peak times give you so much anxiety you'd rather stay home. Or, you just hate grocery shopping — period. Maybe you want to be someone who likes buying food, but if you're not that person now, you probably never will be. Stop fooling yourself and do yourself a favor: Order groceries online.

Look at Food Holistically

I still see people using a meat-veg-potatoes mindset and who want to see these three roughly equal components in every meal. Take fried rice, for example. I get asked what kind of vegetables I eat with it to make a complete meal. I suggest cooking some broccoli (see page 98) or stir-frying broccolini or leafy Chinese greens with a drizzle of oyster sauce over top. Or don't if that's not for you. Roasted Cauliflower with Za'atar (see page 112) is a go-to dish for me when I really don't feel like cooking, but some people see it more as a side. There is more than enough for me if I add some wholewheat pita or flatbread to eat alongside.

Confession: Some evenings I don't eat vegetables. There's certainly one day every week where I'm too tired and just have rice and a fried egg for dinner. Now, I certainly don't want to recommend this, but it works really well for me to look at the big picture instead of forcing myself to eat vegetables with every meal. I'm happy as long as I get enough vitamins on a weekly basis.

Find what works for you personally. For example, I eat a lot of vegetables at lunch. Sometimes by four o'clock, I can sense that I'm going to be tired and lazy in the evening, so I'll snack on a tomato or vegetables that are in the fridge, just to sneak in some extra veg. If you don't work from home, take raw vegetables to work or start the day with a green smoothie.

Cook in Batches

Despite my extensive cooking and food planning, I am very lazy. Fortunately, my laziness is a fantastic source of efficiency and cooking in batches is very efficient. Whether you're cooking potatoes or roasting a cauliflower, it often doesn't take much more effort to prepare a little bit more food, leaving you with something left over.

Nothing beats opening the fridge and seeing some leftover Brothy Beans (see page 124), cooked green beans and herb mash (see page 61). Reheat everything together, add fried egg over top and there's your dinner. Another big advantage to batch cooking vegetables is that all vegetables shrink when you cook them, so they don't take up as much space in the fridge. Sometimes, when my vegetable drawer won't close because of a giant cauliflower, I'll roast it in advance. (Not to mention roasted cauliflower always comes in handy.) If you roast cauliflower with just salt and pepper, you can figure out which flavors to add later. You will also finish semi-prepared ingredients faster than raw ones because there is less to do. Think back to what type of one-person household you are (see page 14). If you're not home much, the semi-prepared food

in those containers can go bad sooner, so don't go overboard with prepping.

You'll find batch cooking even easier if you're like me and have a lifestyle where you're often at home during the day. For example, sometimes when I boil eggs for lunch, I'll add small potatoes in the same water. Or, I'll put on a saucepan of beans for dinner. I prefer to cook a little at different times rather than everything at once because I'm tired by the evening. I understand that this is a privilege and not feasible for everyone. But, maybe the next time you boil water or turn on the oven, you'll find something else you can make at the same time, which will save time the next day. Consider it meal prep for lazy people.

Tips for Leftovers and Throwing Less Away

1. Buy Vegetables That Stay Fresher Longer
Throwing less away starts with smart shopping. If you live alone and often eat out spontaneously, it might not help you much to stuff your fridge full of spinach, mint and bags of salad mix. Save those purchases for when you're sure you'll finish them within two days and focus on products that keep for a long time. Always buy whole vegetables in any case. A whole head of lettuce will always last longer than chopped and bagged. As far as lettuce goes, romaine, little gem and iceberg will stay fresh longer than softer varieties such as butter lettuce. Or use radicchio, Belgian endive or radicchio rosso. Cauliflower, kale, white cabbage, Brussels sprouts, carrot, green beans, flat beans, eggplant, zucchini and winter squash all keep for a long time. Some cabbages will even stay good for up to a

month. Keep in mind that as soon as you cut into things, they start to wilt a little, so keep an eye on it. Sometimes you pick the wrong vegetable and it starts showing brown spots after three days.

I know I said we wouldn't freeze anything in this book, but, if you happen to have a freezer, consider freezing blueberries, spinach and peas. Freezing spinach, in particular, will free up a lot of fridge space and help it keep for longer. If you don't have a freezer, ignore this paragraph.

2. Know How to Store Food
Oh no, you've reached into the back of the veggie drawer and found a slimy, withered cucumber. Knowing how to store fruits and vegetables properly is a big help in keeping them fresh for longer. Eggplants and tomatoes, for example, are best kept on the counter. Spinach and other leafy greens, fresh herbs, endives, Belgian endives, cauliflower, broccoli and sprouts are best stored in the fridge. For a specific guide to storing herbs, see page 58.

Bananas omit gas that ripens fruits faster (and they therefore rot faster). Buy a mesh or basket fruit bowl that lets air circulate around the fruit. This past summer, I had the most beautiful tomatoes, but they kept getting moldy on the bottoms because they didn't get enough air. The same can happen with onions and garlic. Potatoes are best kept in a cool, dark place.

3. Gone Bad? Prepare It!
If you notice your vegetables or fruit turning brown despite all these efforts, prepare them! Cut out the brown spots and roast or cook your vegetables. For example, purée tomatoes and use them as a base for pasta sauce, beans

or a curry. Cook fruit in a saucepan, perhaps with a little sugar, lemon zest, ground cinnamon, ginger, cardamom or pie spices. It's delicious over yogurt or ice cream. Or, make a smoothie. This stops the brown spots from getting bigger on the fruit and it'll keep in the fridge for at least a few days once prepared.

For a while I was addicted to the YouTube series *Budget Eats* by Delish. In the videos, the host, June, took on different challenges that all involved her having to eat on a very small budget for a week. It always started with a shopping haul. June often scored bags of fruit and vegetables in the bargain bin that were about to be removed from the store. Once she got home, her first step was to prep. I couldn't get enough of it. I watched her for hours preparing food and putting everything in containers. I get that not everyone has time to watch June's videos (frankly I don't either), but rewatching a video every now and then always helps my creativity and leftovers mindset. A little "What would June do?" is never a bad thing. *(June later had a falling out with Delish and now has her own channel: Junelikethemonth.)*

4. Put Old Things in View
That cucumber might be slimy because it was all the way down at the bottom of the drawer. Make sure you keep things that are almost expired visible. Incidentally, by that I mean vegetables that don't look so fresh anymore, because I've never complied with a best-before date. I always smell, look and taste. Sometimes I drink milk that is two weeks past its prime, without batting an eyelid. Don't sue me if this doesn't work for you,

but I promise you can relax a bit in terms of best-before dates.

Do check your fridge from time to time (such as before you shop for the week) and bring things to the front that need to be eaten soon. Or, put them on the counter so you know you need to cook them that evening. I very often have two tablespoons of sauce, a few roasted nuts or half an onion lingering in the refrigerator. If I leave them out or front-and-center in the fridge, I won't forget about them. You can usually just throw them into something and for me that usually happens the next morning. Everything tastes good on eggs — it's just a fact.

5. Invest in Good Containers
This builds on the previous point: It's very important to use transparent containers so you can see what's in them. If you want to get serious about it, you could stick tape on the containers identifying what you've cooked, like a real chef, although that's not entirely realistic for me. It really does help to see what's in a container. You're more likely to grab it because it looks more appealing or to remember you have it. Consider glass over plastic and get a range of sizes, ideally ones that stack neatly.

My containers are perhaps more important to me than is healthy. Maybe you don't need to buy a set of seventy containers like I have, but make sure you have some on hand. It saves you money in the long run because you're throwing less away.

6. Forget All the Rules
You've carefully stored all your food in containers. Now what? The first step

to using up leftovers is to forget all the rules. Nothing you've learned about ingredients that go well together or "how it's done" is relevant here. Leftover vegetables from an Italian meal? Probably great on a taco. What about veg with harissa for breakfast? Sure. It's a lot easier to use up leftovers when you stop thinking within defined parameters. Eat pasta sauce over rice the next day. Dilute your curry and turn it into soup. Throw the last bit of dill into your Asian-inspired noodles. Almost everything tastes great, and if it doesn't, then you've learned something. The one rule not to forget is to date your containers and use leftovers within a few days to avoid spoilage.

I'll give you tips on what to do with the leftovers for many of the recipes in this book, but trust your own tastes. The more you try things, the more creative you'll get.

7. Everything Tastes Great on a Sandwich
A trick I use for pretty much all leftover veggies, but also for chunky sauces, is to put it on bread. I eat a lot of toast with cream cheese, ricotta or labneh and the previous day's veggies on top. Or, try making a grilled sandwich.

8. Be Forgiving
Despite giving you all of my tips, I still end up throwing out more food than I'd like. I recently had to toss paneer, ricotta and pomegranate seeds in the garbage in the span of a single week. I was really annoyed at myself, but I'm only human. Do the best you can because every little bit helps.

CAPSULE

KITCHEN

I first heard the term *capsule wardrobe* a few years ago. The idea is to create a small collection of basics that you can vary infinitely. With about twenty to forty pieces of clothing, you should be able to put together a good outfit, no matter the occasion or time of day. I want you to apply the same premise to your kitchen. You don't need a lot of ingredients to achieve wide-ranging flavors.

My capsule kitchen has two components. First, I establish that ten seasonings is enough to cook alone. By seasonings, I mean bottled sauces, vinegars and so on. Lemons and fresh herbs are seasonings, too, but you can buy them weekly, so they don't take up a permanent spot in your fridge or kitchen cabinet. There is nothing more annoying than buying a large amount of an ingredient for a recipe and then have it sit on the shelf unused, getting in the way forever.

I've selected my ten essential flavors for you (see page 24). If you buy these ingredients, you'll be able to make all the recipes in this book and many more. Keep in mind that the flavors you like are very personal. Maybe you don't want to get za'atar at all, but you think miso should be on the list. My advice is always to start with a recipe and get the ingredients to make it. From there you can expand. Remember: Your tastebuds are in charge.

The second part of the capsule kitchen is your capsule pieces. It's the sauces, leftovers and other ready-to-eat items you have on hand to make a meal at any time. Think herb mixes, sauces, some kind of foundation (hummus, yogurt) and a carb of some kind. Often I find myself standing in front of the fridge with no desire to cook, managing to put together a meal by mixing together the components of three containers.

Take, for example, a can of beans combined with some herb mix (see page 61). Stir in some tomato, fry an egg and you've got dinner. Got yesterday's green beans and some plain yogurt? Pour some tahini or chili oil over top, grab a chunk of bread and voilà! You do need to make some of these things in advance, but once you have a fridge that functions well, it's just a question of saving leftover sauces. There are no strict rules for this either, but I'll explain how I do it and give you some easy combinations.

Salt

I'm assuming you have olive oil, mayo and salt on hand. Buy your favorites, but I'd like to say a little something about salt. I always have fine sea salt (my preference is La Baleine) and flaky sea salt (I like Maldon). I use fine sea salt to season as I cook, and coarse sea salt to finish things off. I recommend having both on hand. I tend to stay away from Himalayan salt, smoked salt and flavored salt. They take up space and I ultimately never use them.

Ten Essentials

Over the following pages, I've outlined the ten ingredients you need for a lifetime of good food. I'm not including staples, such as olive oil, mayonnaise, salt and so on. I'm also not counting spices, partly because I consider them interchangeable. There's a lot of cumin, coriander, ground turmeric and sesame seeds in this book. If you'd rather have fennel seed with your Instagrammable eggs (see page 41) or stir nutmeg into your orzo (see page 130), feel free. Work with what you have. If you have four or five favorite spices, that will take you a long way.

Just like with a capsule wardrobe, the quality of the products is important. Try to get the best-quality seasonings available to you.

Tahini
This sesame paste is used a lot in Middle Eastern cuisines, but I stir tahini into everything from Lebanese food to Chinese food, from sweet to savory. I even drizzle a little over top of my oatmeal with fruit. Sesame paste is also used in China, but is quite a bit nuttier and darker. (It can be used as a substitute for tahini in a pinch.) Tahini is great for making spicy sauces just a little creamier and milder. The consistency of tahini can really vary. The stuff in supermarkets and health food stores is often quite dense. If you can, try to buy your tahini at a Middle Eastern grocery store, where it tends to be creamier. If your tahini is very dense, dilute it a bit with warm water.

Alternatives: If you're using tahini in Asian-inspired recipes, peanut butter will work as a substitute. Or, if you happen to have it, try Asian sesame and peanut paste. In a pinch, use whatever nut butter you have on hand. The taste will just be a bit creamier and nuttier. You also may want to dilute the nut butter with water.

Za'atar
Za'atar is one of my favorite ingredients because it has such a complex flavor that you don't often need to use any other spices. It is a Middle Eastern spice blend that is generally a combination of toasted sesame seeds, sumac, dried oregano, marjoram and thyme, although recipes can vary. It is becoming more accessible, but I find the best ones are from Middle Eastern stores. Za'atar is also the name of an herb, a kind of wild oregano that forms the basis of the mixture in dried form. Try it sprinkled over roasted cauliflower, baked potatoes or a fried egg, or stir into olive oil for the tastiest dip for bread or crudités.

Soy Sauce
This condiment is essential to many, many Asian dishes and has a wide range of uses. Soy sauce adds a salty flavor to dishes. There are both light and dark versions available in well-stocked grocery stores. Light soy sauce is saltier and rich, and the dark variety is more syrupy, often added for color. I use the light version in this book (and refer to it as "soy sauce" in the recipes). My favorite kind is Superior Light from Pearl River Bridge, but Kikkoman is good, too, and available at most supermarkets.

Add a dash to stir-fried vegetables with garlic and a light drizzle of toasted sesame oil (see page 29). It's also good mixed into a vinaigrette with olive oil and honey.

Toasted Sesame Oil

Sesame oil is used in a lot of Asian recipes and gives any dish a recognizable nutty flavor. When you're using it, keep in mind that a little goes a long way. Just a teaspoon of toasted sesame oil is enough to turn an entire head of broccoli into something delicious. It is also great in a vinaigrette, a sauce for noodles or for drizzling over congee (see page 85). Always buy toasted sesame oil (or you'll miss out on that nutty goodness) and make sure to check the list of ingredients. It should say "100% sesame." Try to buy it from an Asian grocery store if you can.

Rice Vinegar

I used to buy the exact type of vinegar called for in a recipe. (I must admit that I don't maintain a capsule kitchen myself — my kitchen cabinets are bulging.) Sometimes I was happy with that decision, but when I open the cupboards and see unused bottles of apple cider vinegar and white wine vinegar, I am not. For these reasons, I always fall back on rice vinegar. It's versatile, perfectly acidic, fresh and light, and it has a bit more sweetness and body than white vinegar, for example. It's great in vinaigrettes and sauces and also for pickling onions.

Alternatives: I make a lot of Asian-inspired dishes, which is why I often end up using rice vinegar. If you like to cook a lot of French or Italian dishes, consider using white wine vinegar or white vinegar as your go-to vinegar. People look down on white vinegar because it's the least flavorful of the three types and comes in the least sexy bottle, but I use it second only to rice vinegar. I love it's super-fresh taste. If you make a lot of vinaigrettes, consider investing in a vinegar with more depth, such as red wine or sherry; however, those aren't all-purpose vinegars to the same degree.

Harissa

My fridge is full of spicy red sauces, but if I could only choose one, I'm going with harissa paste. Harissa paste adds a smoky and fiery flavor to dishes and is more earthy and aromatic than something like sambal oelek. I often combine it with some olive oil, garlic and honey to make a quick sauce for vegetables or potatoes, but it's also great for marinating tofu or to mix into ketchup to spread onto a grilled sandwich. I use traditional spicy harissa, but you can always use rose harissa if you can't find it. I'm grateful to Ottolenghi for making rose harissa so popular that it is now available from Middle Eastern grocery stores and some well-stocked supermarkets. It's a bit sweeter and more aromatic.

Alternatives: Sambal oelek, sriracha or gochujang can all be used as substitutes for harissa paste. Sambal and sriracha have a little more tangy kick, while gochujang is funkier and richer. Gochujang is also thicker and more concentrated than the other two, so you'll need less of it, or you'll have to dilute it with oil or water.

Doubanjiang, a Szechuan chili bean paste, is another good way to add instant flavor to food. This paste is fermented and has lots of depth, which means you need it and almost nothing else. Doubanjiang does have a pronounced taste so it's less suitable for use on everything, but it's a fun addition for the right dish.

Furikake

Furikake is a Japanese condiment comprised of seaweed, bonito flakes, sesame seeds and other ingredients. There are many versions of furikake, from wasabi to egg yolk, so try a bunch of different kinds from your Asian grocery store or look for them at your local supermarket. (I prefer the options at Asian grocery stores, but do what you can.) I love liberally sprinkling it over rice or adding it to rice with an egg for a complete meal.

Alternatives: Look out, vegetarians: Furikake very often contains fish flakes. If you don't eat fish, buy vegetarian furikake or substitute for some crumbled gim and toasted sesame seeds.

You can also crumble gim on your rice and add some toasted sesame seeds. Gim is Korean salted seaweed, available from Asian grocery stores and health food stores. I use gim more often, but furikake is more readily available.

Aleppo Pepper

I have a lot of different dried peppers on hand, but I think Aleppo pepper is the best for everyday use. Originally from the Middle East, it's a little milder than hot pepper flakes and has a slightly smoky, almost sweet taste. I like it sprinkled over congee (see page 85).

Alternatives: Hot pepper flakes are more readily available than Aleppo pepper, but keep in mind they are spicier, so use a smaller quantity. Another mild chile pepper option is gochugaru, which are Korean chili flakes. You can find them at Asian grocery stores or well-stocked supermarkets.

Olives

I always have a jar of Taggiasche olives at home. Sprinkle them over mozzarella for a fantastic toast (see page 56). Or, stir them into a simple tomato sauce for pasta or use as a garnish for vegetables. Think green beans are boring? Not with a drizzle of olive oil and some coarsely chopped olives sprinkled over. Kalamata olives are tasty, too. Try to get the best quality available.

Capers

Capers are kind of in the same category as olives for me really and I often use the two together. They're great in a salsa verde or stirred into a potato salad. Or, fry them and sprinkle them on a cracker with mackerel or over tomato salad.

MIX &

MATCH

It's a great relief when you're too tired to open the fridge and discover that you don't have to cook — or don't have to cook much. Having prepared vegetables amounts to hitting the jackpot, but I try to have other ready-to-go options for everything else. In the next few pages, you'll see a list highlighting some different components of a meal (the base, filling, vegetables, sauce and an optional crisp element). I do a bit of a rotation, ensuring I have something from each category at home. This is how I mix and match to make a meal out of the things I already have.

Something as a Base

Make It Yourself
In my opinion, vegetables on a creamy base of labneh, hummus or plain yogurt is a meal. I almost always have labneh (see page 37) or hummus (see page 37) on hand. Both of these recipes do take time (dried chickpeas need to soak and the yogurt for labneh must be drained). If you want something faster, tofu crème (see page 37) is quick — and vegan — too.

Ready to Go
Middle Eastern and well-stocked grocery stores have ready-made labneh. If you don't have time to make labneh, thick Greek, Turkish or Bulgarian plain yogurt is a great accessible alternative. Ricotta, cottage cheese and even cream cheese, in my opinion, will work as a substitute. You can find prepared hummus easily now; look for something that is good quality.

Something Filling

Make It Yourself
I don't know about you, but if I want to avoid a raging hunger after a meal, I need some kind of carbs. If I'm cooking potatoes, I always cook myself an extra serving. They are always good on a little plate (see page 62) or in a potato salad (see page 141). You can also try it as a snack with a dollop of mayo and a caper on top. Cooking beans or chickpeas (see page 124) from scratch are always tastier than canned. I try to make enough for the whole week.

Noodles and spaghetti taste best if you eat them right away, but sometimes I'll also make a double serving of small pasta, such as pearl couscous or orzo. Stir them into your leftover roasted vegetables and you'll — almost — always have a salad. If I'm making flatbread (see page 37), I'll sometimes make a double serving. You can keep the dough in the fridge for at least five days so you can easily have fresh flatbread later.

Ready to Go
Beans, lentils and chickpeas can of course be bought canned. It's helpful to always have some in the cupboard. You can buy bread in all shapes and sizes, depending on your needs. I always have whole wheat pita on hand, too. The only downside is that they are often in large packages, so you do have to finish them fairly quickly if you don't have a freezer. Try baking old pita drizzled with some olive oil and sprinkled with za'atar for a crispy snack.

Some Vegetables

Make It Yourself

Vegetables cooked at home always taste better, whether it's sautéed kale or roasted eggplant. I've said this before, but if you're already planning to cook a small portion of a vegetable, consider cooking all of it, unless you know you won't be eating at home the rest of the week. Prepared vegetables are such a blessing on busy days. Just season your veg with salt and/or pepper so they can be combined in all sorts of ways later in the week.

Ready to Go

I don't have much of a problem not eating vegetables once in a while. If I'm so tired that I can't even throw broccolini in the oven, I'll usually just leave it out. On those days, I'll just have rice with a fried egg or a vegan tuna bowl (see page 82). If you'd like to have some prepared vegetables at home for emergencies, opt for canned corn or precooked beets. I also always have frozen spinach (both chopped and creamed) on hand, but that requires a freezer.

Some Kind of Sauce

Make It Yourself

Everything tastes better with sauce, so it's always a good idea to make extra of whatever sauce you're already preparing. From the harissa dressing on the eggplant caprese (see page 115) to the Love Potion on Crispy Rice with mushrooms (see page 90). The Instagrammable nutty butter on page 41 is great the next day spooned over vegetables or rice.

Ready to Go

I will not recommend buying prepared pestos or salad dressings. While they are convenient, I never find they taste as good as what I can make. If you don't have any homemade sauces on hand, consider adding a glug of good olive oil, a squeeze of lemon and some flaky salt to add flavor. Or, try just adding a dollop of mayo, the queen of sauces.

Bonus: Crisps of Some Kind

Make It Yourself

This is by no means obligatory, but anything crispy instantly makes any dish better. Try sprinkling crispy fried breadcrumbs or panko, shallot or garlic crisps (see page 144) or crunchy seeds (see page 130) over a meal to immediately give you that restaurant feeling.

Ready to Go

Prepared fried onions can help you cut corners here. For more crunch than crisp, buy any type of nut you like and chop them coarsely in advance.

MIX & MATCH EXAMPLES

Combine roasted eggplant (see page 115) with Love Potion (see page 61) and serve over labneh (see page 37) or plain with whole wheat pita or Flatbread (see page 37).

Combine sautéed kale (see page 123), cooked orzo and harissa dressing (see page 115). Finish with crispy seeds (see page 130) and top with a spoonful of plain yogurt.

Top cooked noodles or spaghetti with ginger mushrooms (see page 55) and a Marinated Egg (see page 98).

Spoon hummus onto a plate and finish with drained and rinsed canned corn and sautéed spinach with garlic (see page 123). Serve with toast, Flatbread (see page 37) or pita.

Serve roasted cauliflower (see page 112), pickled radish (see page 82) and tahini mayo (see page 119) in a whole wheat pita or on Flatbread (see page 37).

Combine day-old cooked rice with vinaigrette (see page 141), roasted eggplant and lots of fresh herbs. Serve with a handful of Garlic-Pistachio Crisps (see page 129) or a handful of chopped roasted nuts.

Combine cooked beans or chickpeas (see page 124 or use drained and rinsed from a can) with herb mash (see page 61), tomato or cooked green beans, and a little fried halloumi.

HOW TO
USE

THIS
BOOK

Serves Approximately One Person

All the recipes in this book have been written for one, but I encourage you to make more of the individual components of the dishes: the vegetables, herb mash, sauces and hummus. By now you'll have read why this is important in the Capsule Kitchen chapter (see page 22). If not, you should go back and read it now. You don't want the fridge to be full of leftovers you just throw away later.

More than One Person

If you're in a relationship, you have a family or you're cooking for friends, you can increase the quantities of any recipe as needed, obviously. We singles do that all the time, but in the other direction. In my view, it's always easier to increase than reduce.

Finishing Leftovers the Smart Way

I'll give you options with each recipe for how to transform leftover vegetables or sauces into a whole new meal the next day. I'll also outline a few of my go-to meals that don't require a recipe (see page 34), including my absolute favorite, the little plate (see page 62). Hopefully I'll inspire you to incorporate your leftovers in a fun way, without having to eat the same thing all week long.

In the tips and variations, I may sometimes mention ingredients that are not in the Capsule Kitchen. I'll always keep the original recipe simple, but I want to give you options if you'd like to take it a step further using items you have on hand. That means the book will be useful for you as you're starting out as a solo cook, but also once you already know a few tricks.

Thinking for Yourself

My ultimate dream for you is that over time, you will no longer need this book. That's because cooking for yourself really isn't rocket science — you just need to think a little differently. Being able to cook well is ultimately a matter of confidence: It's the self-assurance to rely on your own taste and adjust the proportions in a recipe a little. It's the confidence to combine things you're not sure go together, which you build through lots of trial and error.

Measurements

I'm not big on precise tablespoons and ounces (or grams), but they're simply unavoidable if you're writing a cookbook. So, all the quantities in this book have been precisely measured by me with measuring spoons and cups or a kitchen scale (when quantities are provided in weights). You know, the measuring spoons and nesting-style dry measuring cups you buy in a set at the kitchen store. For liquids, use a glass or plastic "liquid" measuring cup with a handle and spout. A basic digital kitchen scale is also handy. For ingredients 2 tablespoons and less, metric is not included as I assume you're using a set of measuring spoons marked with tablespoons. In case you want to measure in metric, a teaspoon holds 5 mL and a tablespoon 15 mL.

FREE

STYLE

The podcast I did with my besties Marieke and Brian had a weekly "freestyle" feature about cooking without a recipe. Once you've mastered some basic knowledge and techniques, it's usually not a problem. In fact, I usually improvise when I cook. If I didn't have to create recipes because I write cookbooks, I'd be freestyling every time. The following recipes are those I often eat when I have no time, interest or inspiration, but they're so simple I don't even need to give you recipes for them. They're perfect for practicing your freestyling.

Rice with Egg

Fry one or two eggs and eat them over top cooked rice with a dash of soy sauce, toasted sesame oil and toasted sesame seeds sprinkled on top. Stir a bit of butter into the rice if you're feeling fancy. It's delicious with cooked broccoli topped with a drizzle of toasted sesame oil.

Aglio e Olio

Cook spaghetti in a saucepan of generously salted water. Meanwhile, sauté garlic and hot pepper flakes over low heat in lots of olive oil. Turn off the heat. Drain the pasta and add it to the oil mixture in the skillet. It's not proper, but at this point I always add a bit of butter, which is just delicious. Serve it with lots of Parmesan cheese sprinkled over top. Cooked broccoli with a squeeze of lemon juice and olive oil is great on the side, if you have the energy to cook it.

The Easiest Tomato Sauce

In a small baking dish, combine a large can of tomato paste, a few tablespoons of butter, some garlic cloves and anchovy fillets (optional) and cook for 30 minutes in an oven preheated to 350°F (180°C). Mash everything together using a fork or an immersion blender. Stir into your fave cooked pasta and serve with Parmesan cheese sprinkled over top. It's easy to add leftover veg and protein to tomato sauce to make a satisfying meal.

Whole Wheat Pearl Couscous

Cook whole wheat pearl couscous in a saucepan of generously salted water. Drain and combine with cooked chickpeas, fresh mint, feta, olive oil and lots of black pepper. This is also the perfect to-go salad.

Fish Sticks

Sometimes people laugh at me because they think fish sticks are for kids, but I don't think so. I always have vegetarian fish sticks in the freezer and they're delicious every time I eat them alongside some creamed spinach and baked potatoes or cooked rice. Sometimes I replace the fish sticks with vegetarian chicken nuggets or a vegetarian sausage.

BASIC

RECIPES

Hummus for a Week

Soak ¾ cup (150 g) dried chickpeas overnight in a bowl of cold water. Drain and boil the chickpeas with 1 teaspoon of baking soda in a saucepan with plenty of water. Scoop out the skins that float to the surface from time to time, with a slotted spoon or skimmer. Once the chickpeas are soft (probably after 30 to 40 minutes), drain and pour into a tall cup to use with an immersion blender. Add 1 garlic clove, the juice of 1 lemon, ⅓ cup (80 g) tahini, 1 teaspoon of salt and 3 tbsp + 1 tsp (50 mL) water; blend until smooth and creamy. You may need to add a little bit more water. I usually use 6 tbsp + 2 tsp (100 mL) altogether, but it can vary.

(STORAGE): Covered hummus will keep for up to one week in the fridge; however, it sometimes can turn after just 4 or 5 days. You'll taste the difference immediately (it's tangy).

Labneh for a Week

Combine a pinch of salt with 2 cups (500 g) plain Greek or other thick yogurt. I always just do this in the yogurt container to save on dishes. Spoon the yogurt into a sieve lined with cheesecloth placed over a large bowl. If you don't have cheesecloth, a clean lint-free tea towel is fine, too. Tie a knot in the cloth and let the yogurt drain in the fridge for at least 2 hours but preferably overnight.

(STORAGE): Covered labneh keeps for up to one week in the fridge.

Tofu Crème for a Week

Using an immersion blender, blend 1 block (10 oz/300 g) silken tofu with 1 garlic clove, 1 tablespoon of olive oil, the juice of 1 lemon, plenty of herbs and salt, until smooth. You can use any tender herbs here, but I really like a combination of basil and cilantro. Taste and add more salt if needed.

(STORAGE): The covered tofu crème keeps up to 2 weeks in the fridge.

Flatbread

For one flatbread, combine 6 tbsp + 2 tsp (60 g) whole wheat flour, 1 tablespoon of plain Greek yogurt, 2 teaspoons of olive oil or butter and a pinch of salt in a large bowl. Add just a little more water (about 1 tablespoon) and, using your hands, combine until a smooth ball forms. Let it rest for half an hour. Roll out the dough on a lightly floured surface and cook in a dry skillet over medium heat, about 1 minute each side.

I've tested this recipe, of course, but I just wing it at home. Make the recipe once first, so you know what the dough should feel like. Once you know, you can experiment. Sometimes I leave out the oil or butter and sometimes the yogurt. Sometimes I add yeast and let it rise for a few hours. Sometimes I make it with just water or with half all-purpose flour, half whole wheat flour. Sometimes I make it thicker and sometimes it's thinner; but, believe me, it always tastes great.

Eggs with Instagrammable Nutty Butter

Two boiled eggs on toast is the perfect breakfast, but sometimes you want to impress someone. Maybe it's yourself or maybe you want to take an amazing photo for your friends or online followers. If that's the case, spoon some of this nutty, buttery, golden sauce over your eggs. There's very little extra work involved, but it will make your breakfast moment look and taste better.

2 eggs
Small handful of peeled hazelnuts
Butter
1 tbsp sesame seeds
$\frac{1}{2}$ tsp ground turmeric
Pinch of Aleppo pepper
Salt
Fried Bread (see page 49)
Fresh dill leaves

Boil the water in a medium saucepan. Add the eggs and cook for 5 minutes. (I prefer a runny yolk, so cook the eggs for a bit longer if you'd like them to be firmer.)

Meanwhile, coarsely chop the hazelnuts. Melt a large spoonful of butter in a small skillet over low heat. Watch closely so that you don't burn the butter. Add the hazelnuts, sesame seeds, turmeric, Aleppo pepper and a pinch of salt. Cook for 1 to 2 minutes, until the hazelnuts and sesame seeds are golden. Remove from heat.

Drain the eggs and shock them under cold running water. Then peel and halve the eggs. Place the egg halves on toast and drizzle the hazelnut butter over top. Sprinkle with dill.

(VARIATION): I often eat this on toast, but it's also great over top plain Greek yogurt with some grated garlic stirred in. Eat it with whole wheat pita for dipping.

(STORAGE): Sometimes I think it's a waste to cook just one or two eggs. If you know you'll be eating at home a few more times that week, boil a few more and make the Marinated Eggs on page 98.

Oatmeal or Rice Pudding?

Rice pudding is the perfect food for me. I like it in all forms, from French riz au lait to Indian kheer, from rice custard to sweet Dutch rice pie. This recipe is a life hack to give your breakfast some rice pudding vibes. All credit for this recipe goes to my bestie Marieke, who wanted to make oatmeal one morning but didn't have enough on hand. She did, however, have some leftover sushi rice. Combine the two and you've got a porridge reminiscent of rice pudding! It's not really a dessert, but a little imagination will take you a long way. And if I want dessert, I always have supermarket rice dessert in the fridge for emergencies (see page 158).

$\frac{1}{3}$ cup (30 g) quick-cooking rolled oats
3 tbsp (38 g) cooked rice (preferably short-grain)
1 cup (250 mL) whole milk or plant-based milk
Salt
Butter
1 tbsp dark brown sugar

Combine the oats, cooked rice, milk and a pinch of salt in a small saucepan. Cook on low heat until the ingredients are warm. Ladle into a bowl, top with butter to taste and sprinkle with brown sugar.

(VARIATION): For a healthier option, I often stir a mashed banana into my oatmeal. Just mash it in the saucepan before adding the rest of the ingredients.

Blended Chia-Chocolate Pudding with Tahini

I'm not the best at weekday breakfasts. Every morning, I resolve to eat something good, but before I know it, it's eleven o'clock and my growling stomach tells me I've failed again. I find it very helpful to have something ready in the fridge that I can reach for right away. Unfortunately, my part-Asian stomach can't tolerate a bowl of yogurt, so I often make chia pudding. I prefer to blend the ingredients using an immersion blender to give it a creamier texture, but you can also just stir all the ingredients together. The pudding will keep in the fridge for a few days, so I always make enough for two to three days.

FOR 2 SERVINGS

The night before

¼ cup (48 g) chia seeds

6 tbsp + 2 tsp (100 mL) whole milk or plant-based milk

6 tbsp + 2 tsp (100 g) plant-based plain yogurt or plain Greek yogurt

2 tbsp unsweetened cocoa powder

1 tbsp maple syrup

In the morning

1 tbsp plant-based plain yogurt or plain Greek yogurt

1 tbsp tahini

Flaky sea salt

Combine the chia seeds, milk, yogurt, cocoa and maple syrup in a tall cup to use with an immersion blender. I don't like my chia pudding to be too sweet. If you have a sweet tooth, you can add a bit more maple syrup. Blend all the ingredients for a good long time, until the chia seeds are fully incorporated. Keep blending for longer than you think: an immersion blender will never get things as smooth as a high-powered blender. Scoop the mixture into a container with a lid and refrigerate overnight.

The next day, scoop half of the pudding into a bowl and finish with a dollop of yogurt, tahini and a pinch of flaky sea salt.

(VARIATIONS): You can vary chia pudding infinitely. Use only milk or yogurt, or add cinnamon, matcha powder, grated carrot or rolled oats. Sometimes I'll blend a banana in with the milk to use as a sweetener and leave out the maple syrup. Fruit is always good as a topping, too.

Nothing beats freshly baked bread, soft on the inside and with a crunchy crust. But if you're on your own, it might be hard to eat the entire loaf in a week. As the oat milk–sipping boujie that I am, I buy a sourdough loaf every week. It's crisp and fresh the first day, less so on day four or five. Fortunately, bread that's been fried is one of the tastiest things ever. Always buy unsliced bread, because sliced dries out faster. Cut it as needed, so only the outermost layer will dry out. If you're frying your bread later in the week, place the dried-out outside layer face down in the pan. Problem solved!

How to Make Perfect Fried Bread

Heat a good amount of olive oil in a skillet and place the driest side of the bread face down. The underside of the bread should be submerged. Fry over medium-low heat for a few minutes, until golden brown. Add some more oil if the skillet looks too dry: The bread really needs a good amount of oil to get a nice color. Press down with the back of a spatula so the bread cooks evenly. Cook on just one side for the perfect crunchy/soft ratio.

Tomato Toast with Olive-Caper Mayonnaise

I look forward to tomato season every summer. My grocer is a complete tomato obsessive and sells them only when they're at their best, which is maybe one and a half months out of the year. When the time comes, I'll buy a bag of tomatoes every week and arrange them on toast almost daily, just like everyone else on my Instagram feed. Occasionally, I'll eat a tomato in a salad, but when the tomatoes are really good, I think they really shine on perfectly fried bread with a good dollop of mayo. I came up with this olive-caper mayonnaise because the olives and capers always rolled off the top of my toast every time I would go for the perfect bite! If you chop them and stir them into the mayonnaise, they can't go anywhere.

| ½ large ripe tomato, the tastiest you can find |
| Salt |
| 1 slice of sourdough bread |
| Olive oil for frying |
| 3 tbsp (42 g) mayonnaise |
| 1 tbsp capers |
| Small handful of pitted Taggiasche or Kalamata olives |

Slice the tomato and salt to taste. Let it stand while you prepare the other ingredients.

Pan-fry the bread according to the directions on page 49.

Meanwhile, coarsely chop the capers and olives and stir into the mayonnaise. Let the bread cool down a little before spreading the mayonnaise over top. Place the tomato slices on top of the mayonnaise and serve immediately.

VARIATIONS): My favorite way to serve tomato toast is with homemade mayonnaise combined with finely chopped chives. It's so easy and absolutely heavenly, but I didn't dare write it here as a recipe. Tahini Mayo (see page 119) is good, too, perhaps combined with a pinch of za'atar, or top the tomato with good-quality anchovies. For a green-herbed mayo, combine (or pulse using an immersion blender) dill, chives or basil and mayonnaise. Nigella seeds are also good, if you happened to buy that for the orzo on page 130. My forever crush Eric Kim (recipe developer for *The New York Times* and others, and author of *Korean American*) puts furikake over top.

BONUS POINTS — MAKE YOUR OWN MAYO): Combine 1 pasteurized egg, 1 tablespoon of Dijon mustard, the juice of ½ lemon, 1 cup (250 mL) oil (I usually use half sunflower, half olive) and a pinch of salt in a tall cup to use with an immersion blender. Blend until the sauce comes together and resembles mayonnaise. Taste and add more salt and lemon juice as needed. If it's too thick, dilute the mayo with a little water. It will keep in the fridge in a covered container for up to 4 days.

Grilled Sandwich with Tuscan Kale and Olives

This "recipe" is really just a reminder that you can eat leftovers in a grilled sandwich. I find that soft vegetables, such as the Tuscan kale from my buttery pasta (see page 123), taste the best, but most vegetables will work. Because a grilled sandwich is already fairly greasy, I prefer to stay away from anything too fatty. I also find the pickled onion cuts the fat in there already quite nicely. You can also add green sauce such as Love Potion (see page 61), harissa eggplant (see page 115) or leftover mushrooms (see page 55) after the cheese. Ultimately, this is really just a guide to making the perfect toasted sandwich. What you put in it is entirely up to you. I regularly make a vegan tuna melt with cheese and tomato slices.

(LEFTOVER PICKLED ONION): This sandwich uses half an onion. If you're already pickling, you might as well pickle a little more. It keeps a long time in the fridge and is delicious with salads or a little plate (see page 62), but also with brothy or Indian-inspired beans (see pages 124 or 126).

$1/2$ red onion

2 tbsp white vinegar or rice vinegar

Pinch granulated sugar

Salt

Sliced cheese (I often use mild cheese, such as mozzarella, but good-quality sharp or old Cheddar is tasty, too)

2 slices of bread (maybe sourdough)

10 pitted Taggiasche or Kalamata olives

Leftover Tuscan kale (see page 123)

Olive oil or sunflower oil for frying

Slice the red onion into thin rings and place in a small bowl with the vinegar, sugar and a pinch of salt. Stir and let stand for 10 minutes. Drain off liquid before using.

Place a layer of cheese on a slice of bread. Place the olives over top of the cheese, followed by the Tuscan kale and the pickled onion. Place more cheese on top of the kale and top with the other slice of bread. Heat a layer of oil in a skillet that has a lid. Place the sandwich in the skillet and cook over low heat with the lid on until the cheese on the bottom slice melts and the bread is golden brown. Covering the skillet ensures you have nice melty cheese.

Turn the sandwich over very carefully and fry the other side. I usually take the lid off for the last minute, so the sandwich doesn't get too soggy. A grilled sandwich usually takes about 10 minutes to cook properly. The bread needs to be perfectly golden brown on the outside and the cheese has to melt around the other ingredients. It takes some time. If needed, turn the sandwich — carefully! — a few more times to get the perfect browned color on both sides. If you have a wire rack, place it over a plate and let the sandwich drain on it. Otherwise, place two chopsticks or knives on a cutting board and put the sandwich on those. This lets steam escape from the sandwich and keeps it crunchy. Let it cool for about 1 minute, cut in half and eat.

52

Ginger Mushrooms on Toast

Mushrooms on toast is justifiably a classic. I love making it with lots of butter or a splash of cream. But I think the best way to highlight the earthiness of mushrooms is to combine them with lots of spices or something very zesty, like ginger. Even people who don't like mushrooms might enjoy the contrasting flavors here. Why not try it? It's delicious alongside a fresh salad with a simple vinaigrette (see page 141).

$1/2$-inch (1 cm) piece of fresh gingerroot

7 oz (200 g) mushrooms of your choice

Olive oil for frying

Salt

1 tsp rice vinegar

Butter

Freshly ground black pepper

Lemon zest

1 slice of sourdough bread

4 tsp chopped fresh parsley or another tender herb

Chop the ginger as finely as possible. Set aside.

If the mushrooms are dirty, wipe them down with a clean cloth. If they are very large, cut them into bite-size pieces. Heat a few tablespoons of oil in a skillet over high heat. Add the mushrooms and a pinch of salt; cook, stirring often, until starting to brown. How fast the mushrooms cook depends somewhat on the type. Add the ginger and cook for a few minutes, until nicely browned. Drizzle the vinegar over the mushrooms and cook until it evaporates. Remove from heat, and add butter to taste and a few twists of pepper; stir. Add lemon zest to taste and salt, if needed.

Fry the bread according to the directions on page 49. Spoon the mushrooms onto the toast, finish with parsley and zest some more lemon over top.

(LEFTOVER MUSHROOMS): Mushrooms are typically something I buy on impulse and then forget about because they're not really part of my regular routine. My favorites are oyster mushrooms and if I have any extras lying around that I haven't cooked, I like to toss them with shawarma spices, salt and olive oil, then bake them in the oven until crispy. Add garlic sauce, pita, iceberg lettuce, cucumber and tomato and you have a delicious meal. Mushrooms are also wonderful when combined with beans (see page 124), in a buttery pasta (see page 123) or over Crispy Rice (see page 90).

Buffalo Mozzarella

This is the sandwich I eat most often from this chapter. The saltiness of the capers and the freshness of the lemon zest is the best thing you can add to mozzarella, in my books. I actually like this more than my beloved caprese sandwich. I don't give you quantities here because you can eyeball what works for you.

1 slice of sourdough bread

Olive oil for frying

Capers

Pitted Taggiasche or Kalamata olives

Buffalo mozzarella

Lemon zest

First, fry the bread according to the directions on page 49.

Coarsely chop the capers and olives. Tear the mozzarella into pieces and place it on the toast. Garnish with capers, olives and lemon zest.

VARIATION : These ingredients are also delicious spread over focaccia or ciabatta.

HERBS

Fresh herbs are a great way to elevate a dish. I scatter them generously and prefer to use a mix of soft herbs. I always have at least three different herbs on hand and tend to alternate between parsley, dill, chives, basil, mint and cilantro. I buy them at my local market or a Middle Eastern grocery store, because you get the best value for money there (read: huge bunches). The only drawback of these huge bunches is that you have to finish them all yourself. That can be hard to do, no matter how enthusiastically you scatter them.

To keep these huge bunches as fresh as possible, take the elastic off as soon as you get home. Check for any bruised or wilted leaves and throw them away immediately, since they can cause the rest of the bunch to go off sooner. Wash the herbs, shake off any excess water and dab them thoroughly with paper towels or a clean tea towel. Keep them in an airtight sealable bag or a container with a piece of paper towel inside it. Moisture causes herbs to wilt and the paper towel can absorb it.

Herb bunches can sometimes keep for up to two weeks, especially if you continue to check for new wilted bits and throw them out. To be honest, I don't always do this (I told you I was lazy!), but every time I do, it really makes a difference and I resolve to always do it going forward.

Mint, however, I treat a bit differently; otherwise, it wilts in a day. Into a large glass or tall plastic container, pour a little layer of sugar water (heat up equal parts sugar and water until the sugar dissolves, then let it cool). Pick the bottom leaves off the stems and place the bunch in the water. Cover with a small plastic bag or loosely close the container lid. Mint will keep for three or four weeks this way.

Storing Herbs

I do a fridge check when I'm putting things away from my weekly shop. This means taking wilted herbs out of the vegetable drawer and using them to make a green mash. If you combine the herbs with fat (olive oil or mayo), they'll stay good for easily another seven to ten days.

I don't want to give you a recipe here because your quantity of herbs will vary every time. Use your best judgment; add the wilted herbs to a container and drizzle a little oil over top. Continue adding oil until you reach your desired consistency. I often make these herb mashes fairly thick because I really see them as a base for my meals. Thick sauce is great on toast, but if you add more oil or some vinegar, you can use it as a dressing for vegetables or salad.

Fried Herbs

Another great way to bring new life to floppy herbs is to fry them. Heat a layer of olive oil or sunflower oil in a wok or skillet over medium-high heat and fry a good handful of any herb until crispy.

(INGREDIENTS): herbs, oil

Herbed Mayo

An instant upgrade to your sandwich! Using an immersion blender in a tall cup, blend the herbs and prepared mayonnaise. You can also chop the herbs very finely and stir them into the mayonnaise, too.

(INGREDIENTS): herbs, mayonnaise

Salsa Chimi

This is kind of a mashup of salsa verde and chimichurri. Although both have tangy vinegar-bases, they're also quite different. Italian-style salsa verde is often made with parsley, basil, capers and anchovies. I make chimichurri using cilantro, parsley, oregano and shallots. I often make a bit of a mix using what I have on hand and what I feel like eating. The only drawback to a green sauce with acidic ingredients is that the herbs discolor faster, which makes them less tasty. Plan to eat the sauce quickly or make it without the vinegar or citrus and add that at the last minute.

(INGREDIENTS): herbs, olive oil, garlic, salt, vinegar or lemon juice or lime juice

(OPTIONAL): finely chopped anchovy or shallot

Love Potion

My mother would always make a purée of basil, olive oil, garlic and salt when we were on vacation in Italy. She called it Love Potion — a kind of lazy person's pesto. This is the green mash I make most, because it's so basic. It's a delicious spread on crackers, but you can add it to all sorts of things.

(INGREDIENTS): herbs, olive oil, garlic, salt

LITTLE
PLATES

A little plate is my version of girl dinner —
the TikTok trend where people (mostly
women) put together a dinner for one
comprised of random items or snacks
found in their kitchen. Sometimes it's
some crackers, olives, a bag of chips and
a tomato; other times it's pasta with
a whole lot of melted cheese. It may
not always be the most nutritious, but
I am very much aligned with the idea of
embracing spontaneity when it comes
to food. Not every meal needs to be pre-
planned and complete; sometimes it's
enough to just cobble it together from
what you have.

By now, friends (and Instagram followers)
know exactly what I mean when I say I've
had a little plate. The only rule is that no
more than one thing can be cooked and the
rest are prepared and/or leftovers. It's good
if you can have a vegetable, a carb and a
protein, but it's not obligatory. This is by no
means just for women. Anyone can eat this
way as long as you're happy with a random
collection of items on a plate.

FIVE PERFECT LITTLE PLATES

Boiled small potatoes + sardines or another canned fish + crème fraîche + little gem lettuce + lemon zest + fresh or fried herbs (see page 61)

Toast + leftover Tuscan kale (see page 123) + butter + tomato sprinkled with lots of black pepper + piece of cheese

Cucumber + tomato + walnuts + feta cheese + green grapes + Flatbread (see page 37) or pita (these are components of a typical Iranian breakfast, so I like to call it a Persian-inspired little plate)

Crackers + hummus (see page 37) + boiled egg + hot pepper flakes + red endive + seed crisps (see page 130)

Roasted cauliflower + tomato + cucumber + za'atar + hummus + bread

GREASY FING
RS GREASY F
REASY FINGE
GREASY FING
RS GREASY F
REASY FINGE
GREASY FING
RS GREASY F
REASY FINGE
GREASY FING

The cocktail hour is not as much of a fixture in my one-person household as I've seen with some couples I know. If I'm over at a couple's place around 5 p.m., I may just suddenly be offered beer and cocktail nuts. I wouldn't think of doing that so readily. I don't know if that's related to my marital status or the fact that I like to eat dinner early. Or, maybe it's because I drink alcohol at home. If I start to get hungry by the end of the afternoon, I usually just start cooking dinner and skip snack time. Nevertheless, making snacks for one can be pretty complicated.

If I happen to be in a snacky mood on the weekend, it can be tricky finding the perfect salty bites at the supermarket. Chips, Japanese party mix or the aforementioned cocktail nuts all turn chewy after a few days, so if you open a bag of something, you'll have to finish it pretty quickly. The snacks in this chapter are perfect for an evening on your own.

The snacks in this chapter are perfect for an evening on your own.

Dilly Pancake with Yogurt Dip

One of my favorite snacks is Taiwanese or Chinese cong you bing, often translated into English as "scallion pancake" or "green onion pancake." It's really a very flaky flatbread layered with green onion and oil. When I've traveled to Taiwan, in particular, I've always gorged myself on them — there are so many varieties using egg, Thai basil, ground beef and the tastiest sauces. When I'm back home, I can find them in the frozen section of my Asian supermarket, but they're actually quite easy to make yourself. This version, however, contains no green onion: I've applied the scallion pancake technique, but used other ingredients.

Since singles are often left with surplus herbs (see page 58), I wanted to create a recipe that would help use them all up. In this case, it's dill, but you could probably use any type of soft herb (or a mix of herbs). I use a small handful of dill here, but feel free to add lots and lots if you like.

(SCALLION PANCAKE): If you're curious about making a scallion pancake, use ¾ cup (100 g) all-purpose flour (omitting the whole wheat flour), leave out the spices and replace the herbs with thinly sliced green onion. Make a dip using a combination of soy sauce, rice vinegar and sesame seeds.

(DIP VARIATION): Harissa paste mixed into the yogurt dip is good, too. If you have sriracha sauce, you can squeeze some right over the pancake and skip the yogurt dip.

(SPICE VARIATION): There are endless spice variations for the oil mixture. Ground cinnamon, ground cumin, ground coriander or whole nigella seed would be tasty, too.

⅓ cup (50 g) whole wheat flour

6 tbsp (50 g) all-purpose flour, plus more for rolling

Salt

1 tbsp olive oil

½ tsp ground turmeric

½ tsp Aleppo pepper

1 tbsp toasted sesame seeds

Big handful of chopped fresh dill leaves

Flaky sea salt

Sunflower oil for frying

3 tsp + 1 tsp (50 g) plain Greek yogurt

Small garlic clove or ½ garlic clove, grated

Combine the whole wheat flour, all-purpose flour and a pinch of salt in a large bowl. Add 4 tbsp + 2 tsp (70 mL) water and knead into a ball. Cover with a damp cloth or plastic wrap and let it rest for at least 30 minutes or up to 4 hours.

Meanwhile, combine the olive oil, ground turmeric, Aleppo pepper and sesame seeds in a small bowl. Coarsely chop the dill.

Dust the counter with some all-purpose flour and roll the dough out into a circle 6 to 8 inches (15 to 20 cm) in diameter. Brush the oil mixture onto the dough and sprinkle dill and flaky sea salt over top. Tightly roll up the dough like a cigar. Starting at one end, roll it up again from left to right, into a kind of spiral. Place one spiral side down and flatten the dough slightly into a disk with your hand, then roll it out again into a circle. If it's tough going, you can let the dough rest for another 5 to 10 minutes, which will make it more pliable.

Heat a generous layer of sunflower oil in a skillet over medium heat and cook the pancake for a few minutes per side, until crisp and golden brown.

Meanwhile, combine the yogurt, garlic, a pinch of salt and perhaps some more herbs in a bowl. Add a tiny bit of water to make the sauce a little runnier. Remove the pancake from the skillet, cut into wedges and serve with the dip.

Popcorn Three Ways

For me, popcorn is the ultimate one-person snack: It stays good for a really long time; it's super cheap; and you can infinitely play with flavors. I'm giving you three options here, but I encourage you to experiment. Furikake is good and so is garlic butter or za'atar. I've tested the flavor options on this page using $\frac{1}{4}$ cup (50 g) popping corn, which gives you a reasonably sized bowl of popcorn. However, I regularly make too much and wind up on the couch with a huge bowl on my lap, which is no hardship.

Making Popcorn

Heat 1 tablespoon of oil in a large, heavy saucepan over medium heat. Add $\frac{1}{4}$ cup (50 g) popping corn and perhaps a pinch of salt. Stir to coat the corn in oil and cover the saucepan. Wait patiently for the whole thing to start popping.

Shake the saucepan every now and again, but do not remove the lid. As soon as you hear little or no popping, the popcorn is ready. For classic popcorn, add butter and some salt to taste or try any other flavor you like. It's best to add butter after cooking: If you pop the corn in butter, it may burn.

Ranch Dressing

After popping the corn, season it with butter and salt to taste, and add 2 teaspoons of dried dill and 2 teaspoons of garlic powder.

Pizza

After popping the corn, season it with $\frac{1}{4}$ cup (25 g) grated Pecorino or Parmesan cheese, $1\frac{1}{2}$ teaspoons of dried oregano and 1 heaping teaspoon of garlic powder. There's no need to add salt because the cheese is already salty. Eat it while it's hot; otherwise, the cheese will harden again and it won't taste good. If you're vegan, replace the cheese with nutritional yeast flakes.

Caramel-Cinnamon

Melt $\frac{1}{4}$ cup (50 g) granulated sugar with a dash of water in a large saucepan. Cook over medium heat, gently swirling the pan, until combined and browned. Pay attention because you don't want the sugar to burn. Once it is a nice caramel color, remove from the heat and add a tablespoon of butter, 3 tablespoons (45 mL) heavy or whipping (35%) cream, a pinch of ground cinnamon and a pinch of salt. Add the popcorn to the saucepan and stir gently to combine. Spread it out on a baking sheet lined with parchment paper so the caramel hardens. Finish with another pinch of flaky sea salt once you're ready to eat it.

Hot Honey Peanuts

Nuts are a great snack for us singles, because they stay fresh for a while once opened. Salted cashews or peanuts (I know, peanuts aren't nuts, but let's say they are for our purposes) are really a treat in themselves. Cocktail nuts, the ones with a crunchy outside layer, are a huge weakness of mine. Hot honey is nothing more than honey mixed with something spicy and it has conquered the Internet as of late. The combination is addictive and tastes good on everything, including peanuts. If you like the hot honey, make a jar of the stuff. Triple or quadruple this recipe and store in an airtight container — just don't add any nuts.

3 tbsp (60 g) honey

1 tbsp granulated sugar

1 tsp hot pepper flakes

1 tbsp spicy harissa paste

$\frac{1}{2}$ tsp rice vinegar

1 cup + 6 tbsp (200 g) salted peanuts

Combine the honey, granulated sugar, hot pepper flakes, harissa paste and rice vinegar in a saucepan over medium heat. Cook until the honey mixture bubbles for 1 minute and is warmed through. Add the peanuts and stir to coat. Spread the peanuts on a baking sheet lined with parchment paper and let them cool. The nuts will be fairly sticky. You can break them into small pieces before serving, if you prefer.

(LEFTOVER PEANUTS): Maybe you won't eat this many peanuts all at once, but once you're cooking, you might as well consider making a bit extra, so double or triple the recipe. The nuts will keep for a few weeks at least.

(LEFTOVER HOT HONEY): Hot honey is also good drizzled over popcorn (see page 70) or ice cream. A suggested flex for a big lunch or dinner: Make a hole in a mountain of butter, pour the hot honey over it and spread it on toast.

Vegetable Fritters

This recipe lets you make something tasty out of all your leftover vegetables. I was inspired by perkedel jagung from Indonesia and pakora from India.

I add spices to the batter as is done with pakora, but the texture of the final dish more closely resembles perkedel jagung. If you don't have any of the spices, you can leave them out and the fritters will still be amazingly good.

1 egg

1 tbsp all-purpose flour

1 tbsp cornstarch

1/2 tsp ground cumin

1/2 tsp chili powder

1/2 tsp ground coriander

1/3 cup (15 g) fresh cilantro sprigs

1 green onion

1 shallot

5 oz (150 g) vegetables (here: corn, carrot, cabbage)

Salt

Sunflower oil for frying

In a bowl, combine the egg, flour, cornstarch, ground cumin, chili powder and ground coriander.

Finely chop the cilantro, including the tender stems. Cut the green onion into 2-inch (5 cm) pieces and cut those pieces into thin strips. Finely chop the shallot. Do what you like with the vegetables. Corn can be drained and added to the batter; carrot and cabbage should be cut into thin strips. I like strips better than finely chopped because you get pointy bits that become extra crispy when fried. Most vegetables can be cut into strips, but something like a leftover boiled potato should be diced into small pieces. Stir the cilantro, green onion, shallot and vegetables into the batter; season with salt.

Heat a generous layer of sunflower oil in a wok or skillet over medium heat. Working in batches as necessary, scoop balls of batter into the oil using two spoons. Flatten the fritters with the back of a spoon and fry for a few minutes, until crunchy and golden brown. Flip and cook until golden on the other side and hot in the center. Drain on paper towels and serve.

(VARIATIONS): Perkedel jagung is eaten without a dip, but various dips might be good with it, of course. Any leftover Love Potion (see page 61) or the yogurt dip for the dilly pancakes on page 69 would work nicely here. If you want to make a quick green chutney, combine some puréed mint, green chile and lime juice.

DELIVERY FOR ONE

One thing is certain when you live alone: There is never a hot meal waiting for you at the end of a busy day — unless you order one. Unfortunately, ordering for one is not as easy as ordering for a group. In many Asian and Middle Eastern cuisines, for example, dishes are meant to be shared. If I order from my favorite Indian restaurant, I want saag paneer, rice but also naan, and a samosa would be good, too. Now that's enough for three people!

Some restaurants offer set menus that are often intended for sharing. This is often still more than you can manage on your own. If you like leftovers and don't mind spending the extra money, consider some of these options. However, I'd rather order food I can eat all at once.

If you want to eat different things, focus on sides. Three side dishes can often make a really good meal for one. When I order Chinese food, I will sometimes only get dumplings. It's dim sum for one. Be sure to check the minimum order amount if you're getting delivery — it varies by restaurant. Very often I think I've got the perfect order, but when I go to pay, I see that I haven't ordered enough or have to pay a bit extra for a small order, which is why I usually fall back on ordering the same things. I've listed my favorites below.

PIZZA:
An Italian pizza with a thin crust is something I can finish in one sitting.

ROTI:
I love vegetarian roti.

McDONALD'S:
Haters gonna hate, but a meal deal is the perfect meal for one.

SANDWICHES:
A falafel, sabich, gyro (vegan, if you don't eat meat), doner kebab (donair) or shawarma is the perfect serving size for me. If you're a bigger eater than I am, you can always order fries, too.

I'm often told that I've changed people's lives because now they cook rice "my" way. As much as I'd like to take credit for their improved quality of life, I did not invent the way to cook rice. The information I'm about to provide will be completely unnecessary to people who have a rice cooker or grew up eating a ton of rice, but there are still a lot of people who cook their rice in lots of water and then drain it. This is for you, darlings.

How to Cook Rice

I always use jasmine rice (which may be called pandan rice at Asian grocery stores). You can also cook basmati rice this way.

Start by measuring your rice: I usually use about $\frac{1}{2}$ cup (100 grams), although you can measure as much rice as you want. Rinse the rice in a sieve under cold running water until the water runs clear. Put the rice in a small saucepan and add one-and-a-half times as much water as rice by volume. Measure the water using the cup you used for the rice, so 2 cups of rice means 3 cups of water. My Indonesian relatives are more laissez-faire about it

and apply the rule that water should be one fingertip above the rice. I sometimes fail using this method, so I always measure it, which is more foolproof.

Place the lid on the saucepan and bring the rice and water (with perhaps a pinch of salt) to a boil over high heat. I used to put the lid on just as the water was boiling, but I read in a Chinese cookbook that this lets the soul of the rice evaporate and I don't want to risk that anymore. Once the water boils, reduce the heat to low. Cook the rice until all the water has evaporated, usually 10 to 15 minutes. Remove from the heat and let the rice stand, covered, for another 10 minutes. Fluff with a fork.

How to Cook Short-Grain Rice

Japanese (sushi) rice is the most readily available type, but Taiwanese is my favorite. Short-grain rice needs less water. Use a rice-to-water ratio of 1 to 1 for short-grain rice instead of 1 to $1\frac{1}{2}$.

All this said, it's always a good idea to check the rice package for directions in case you need a different ratio of water or a longer cooking time.

As much as I'd like to take credit for their improved quality of life, I did not invent the way to cook rice.

Rice Bowl for Lazy People

I make this dish when I really don't know what I feel like, mostly because you don't need to cook anything other than rice. You do, however, need one slightly-hard-to-get ingredient (which is something I promised wouldn't be the case in this book).

When I was recording a TV show in South Korea, the crew went to get breakfast together every day and we could choose from Western or Korean options. I always chose Korean, more specifically a gimbap roll. It's rice, vegetables and some form of protein, rolled in seaweed. The classic version always contains danmuji, which is yellow pickled radish.

If I'm feeling lazy, I'm not going to make an entire roll from scratch. I'll make a rice bowl with as few ingredients as possible that reminds me of the flavors of gimbap. As far as I'm concerned, danmuji is essential. You can buy danmuji premade at Asian grocery stores and it keeps for an incredibly long time. It's worth the trip to buy it because it'll keep for a couple months and then you can always make this super-lazy rice bowl.

(VARIATIONS): If you have more energy, sauté some spinach and then add a drizzle of toasted sesame oil and some raw garlic. Or, sauté some shredded carrot. Both of these vegetables often go into a gimbap roll.

I often eat this rice bowl with leftover vegetables, such as cooked broccoli or sautéed kale. If your veggies are in big pieces, dice them so it's easy to eat with a spoon.

1/2 cup (100 g) short-grain (Japanese) rice

1 3/4 oz (50 g) danmuji

1 3/4 to 2 oz (50 to 60 g) canned tuna or vegan tuna, drained

Generous tablespoon of mayonnaise, preferably Japanese Kewpie

A few tablespoons of furikake or 1 package (0.14 oz/5 g) gim (see page 26)

Cook the rice as described on page 81 or according to package directions. Note: Short-grain rice needs less water than long-grain (equal quantities of rice and water, so 100 milliliters).

Cut the danmuji into 1/2-inch (1 cm) cubes. Scoop the cooked rice into a bowl and top it with the danmuji and tuna. Garnish with mayonnaise and as much furikake as you want. Or, instead of furikake, crumble a package of gim onto the rice using your hands (it's the Korean way). You do you.

(PICKLED VEGETABLES): If you don't feel like going to the store, you can also pickle quartered radishes or diced cucumber. In a saucepan, heat 1/2 cup (125 mL) white vinegar or rice vinegar, 1/2 cup (125 mL) water, 1/4 cup (50 g) granulated sugar, 1 teaspoon of ground turmeric and 1 1/2 teaspoons of salt and cook until the sugar and salt have dissolved. Pour the hot pickling liquid over the cucumber or radish in a bowl and let it cool to room temperature. The pickled vegetables will be ready to eat as soon as they have cooled and will keep in the fridge in an airtight container for at least a few weeks.

Congee with Buttery Corn

For a long time, congee (Chinese savory rice porridge) was my go-to meal after exercising. I would prepare the congee the night before or during the day, so I only needed to heat it up when I was ready to eat. Reheat it on the stove on the lowest-possible heat while you take a shower (this only applies if you take quick showers). I'll also boil an egg while I'm in the shower. Stir in cubes of silken tofu, top with green onion and fried onion and you're done. The buttery corn comes together in less time than it takes to boil an egg, but you can't, unfortunately, do it while you're in the shower.

(VARIATIONS): Pretty much everything is good on congee, even harissa eggplant (see page 115) or roasted cauliflower (see page 112). You can add more flavor to the rice by adding Shaoxing rice wine, a dash of soy sauce, your favorite homemade stock (no stock cubes, please), cooked ground pork or shrimp.

(CONGEE USING LEFTOVER RICE): You can also make congee out of leftover rice. Add a few more cups of water, bring it to a boil and let it simmer over very low heat until you achieve the desired consistency.

(LEFTOVER CORN): Along with broccolini, corn is the only vegetable I add to fried rice. If I have any leftover canned corn, I'll add it to fried rice later in the week or make the Vegetable Fritters on page 74. You can also cook a whole can of corn following the method in this recipe, just increase the quantity of the butter, green onion and ginger. I love it the next day on labneh or bread.

Rice

⅓ cup (60 g) jasmine rice
Salt
1 green onion
1 tsp grated fresh gingerroot
1 cup + 2 tbsp (150 g) drained canned or thawed frozen corn kernels
3 tbsp (42 g) butter
Pinch of Aleppo pepper

SOME OF MY FAVE TOPPINGS

- Soft-boiled egg or marinated egg (see page 98)
- Chili crisp
- Shallot Crisps (see page 144)
- Green onion and/or fresh cilantro
- Pickled cucumber (see page 82)
- Pickled Chinese vegetables and century egg (not for beginners, but classically Chinese and my favorite)

Rinse the rice in a sieve under cold running water until the water runs clear. Combine the rice with 2 cups (500 mL) water and a pinch of salt in a medium saucepan and bring to a boil. Turn the heat to low and let it simmer very gently for 35 to 45 minutes, stirring occasionally. You may want to add more water: I like my congee to be quite runny, but some might prefer it a bit thicker. Decide what you like.

Meanwhile, mince the green onion and combine it with the ginger in a small bowl. Set aside. Once the congee is ready, put the corn, butter, green onion and ginger in a small skillet over low heat. Season with salt and a pinch of Aleppo pepper. Let everything simmer briefly until the green onion and the ginger are aromatic but still fresh, not browned.

Taste the congee and season as necessary with more salt (you need quite a bit of salt, especially if you're not using stock). Ladle the congee into a bowl and spoon the buttery corn over top.

Tofu Salad with Quick Chili Oil

This dish is great when the weather is hot and you don't feel like sweating over the stove for a long time. It works well with any vegetables you have on hand. (Broccolini is a particularly nice addition.) If you don't have time to make your own chili oil, use prepared chili crisp. However, keep in mind that making chili oil from scratch will only take as long as your rice takes to cook and having homemade chili oil around is never a bad thing. Try to use good-quality tofu, since you're eating it raw.

4 oz (125 g) firm tofu

$1/4$ English cucumber

Salt

$1/2$ cup (100 g) jasmine rice

1 tbsp soy sauce

2 tbsp chili oil (see below) or chili crisp

1 tsp rice vinegar

$1/2$ tsp granulated sugar

1 tsp toasted sesame oil

1 tsp grated fresh gingerroot

1 green onion

Small handful of fresh cilantro leaves

Cut the tofu and cucumber into $1/4$-inch (0.5 cm) cubes. Add a pinch of salt, stir and let stand while you prepare the rest of the recipe. This will give them plenty of flavor.

Cook the rice according to the directions on page 81.

In a bowl, combine the soy sauce, chili oil, rice vinegar, sugar, sesame oil and ginger. Add the tofu and cucumber; stir to combine. Taste and add more salt if needed.

Thinly slice the green onion and finely chop the cilantro. Spoon the rice into a bowl and top with the tofu salad followed by the green onion and cilantro. Don't worry if you are out of either green onion or cilantro: The recipe will still be great with just one of them.

(HOMEMADE CHILI OIL): Combine 3 tablespoons (45 mL) hot pepper flakes, 1 teaspoon salt and $1/2$ teaspoon granulated sugar in a small heatproof bowl. Heat $1/3$ cup (75 mL) sunflower oil in a small saucepan. Once the oil is hot, pour it into the bowl so the ingredients start bubbling; stir to combine. Add 1 tablespoon soy sauce and let cool before using. Homemade chili oil will keep for months in the fridge.

(OPTIONAL): This is a very basic chili oil. For added flavor, you could also add star anise, ground cumin, a cinnamon stick or cloves during the first step. Or stir in shallot crisps (see page 144).

(LEFTOVERS): This will make more chili oil than you need for this recipe, but you can add chili oil to everything. I like it on scrambled eggs for breakfast, on congee (see page 85), in noodles or straight on top of fried tofu or any vegetables. Combine it with some more soy sauce to make a dip for dumplings.

(LEFTOVER TOFU? MAKE VEGAN MAYO): Combine 4 oz (125 g) tofu, 1 large tablespoon of Dijon mustard, 3 tbsp + 1 tsp (50 mL) olive oil, 3 tbsp + 1 tsp (50 mL) sunflower oil, the juice of half a lemon and plenty of salt and pepper in a tall cup and use an immersion blender to process until smooth. Taste and add more lemon juice or salt, as necessary.

Golden Fried Rice with Broccolini

Even though I'm on my own, I always make rice for two, so that I can quickly make fried rice when I'm lacking inspiration. I often think it's a waste to put vegetables, like cabbage, in fried rice. I think they can get "lost" in the rice, with no clear distinction between the rice and the vegetables, which doesn't appeal to me. The only exceptions for me are corn and broccolini. They cook quickly, they don't make the rice moist and they don't disrupt the texture of the rice. Golden fried rice is a Chinese technique in which an egg yolk is mixed into the rice. Because the fat of the yolk ends up between the grains, the rice ends up nice and loose, which is what you want in fried rice. You can also achieve this effect with Japanese Kewpie mayonnaise, which is made using only egg yolks.

(VARIATIONS): You almost don't need a recipe for fried rice once you get the hang of the technique. It's so versatile. Add a shallot or any other vegetables. You may also be less particular than me about the consistency of the rice. I sometimes add gochujang (Korean hot pepper paste) and mozzarella to make spicy, cheesy fried rice. Shrimp is a great addition, too. Garnish with fried onion or chili oil (see page 86).

(I LOVE MSG): I always make rice with MSG, but since I didn't include it in the Capsule Kitchen, I omitted it from the recipe. If you have it, add a pinch. It provides a fantastic flavor and has shaken off its bad reputation in recent years.

2 garlic cloves

1 green onion

5 oz (150 g) broccolini

2 eggs

$1^2/_3$ cups (300 g) cooked rice, cooled

Salt

Sunflower oil for frying

Pinch of granulated sugar

Finely chop the garlic and cut the green onion into thin rings. Keep the white and green parts separate. Thinly slice the broccolini stems on the bias. Leave the florets intact. Separate the yolk and white of one egg. Combine the yolk and the cooled rice. In a bowl, whisk together the remaining egg white and the other whole egg. Add a pinch of salt; stir. Make sure everything is prepared before you turn on the stove: The recipe comes together quite quickly once you start cooking.

Heat a few tablespoons of sunflower oil in a wok or skillet over medium-high heat; sauté the garlic and the white part of the green onion for 30 to 60 seconds, until the garlic is aromatic but not browned. Add the broccolini stems and florets and cook for 1 minute. Add the rice, stir to combine and press it into the wok in a single layer. Let the rice cook for 1 to 2 minutes, until warm and crunchy; flip it over. Season with sugar and salt and cook, stirring, for another minute.

Push the rice to the side of the wok, add another dash of oil and pour in the beaten egg. Cook, stirring constantly, until the egg is almost fully scrambled. Combine the egg and rice. Remove from the heat, stir in the remaining green onion and serve.

Crispy Rice

This might be my favorite way to use up leftover rice. Dump the rice into a skillet, press well, cook in a generous amount of oil and you'll end up with an extra-crispy exterior and a nice and fluffy interior. The combination is heavenly. This recipe is nothing new: Many cultures highly covet that crunchy bit at the bottom of the skillet. Think Iranian tahdig or clay pot rice from Hong Kong.

The difference with this recipe is that you need way less skill. For tahdig or clay pot rice, you need good heat control and timing to ensure the rice gets evenly cooked and crispy. In my version, you're just frying up previously cooked rice.

Crispy rice

Sunflower oil for frying

1²/₃ cups (300 g) cooked rice, cooled

Butter

Serve with

1 serving of Ginger Mushrooms (see page 55)

1 tbsp Love Potion (see page 61)

1 tbsp crème fraîche

Lemon zest to taste

Heat a generous layer of oil in a skillet (preferably a small one so you can make a nice disk, but a big one is fine) over medium-high heat. Loosen the rice with a fork and scoop into the skillet. Press the rice down with a spatula so the bottom really sticks together. Cook the rice for 10 minutes, until golden brown and crunchy on the underside. It takes longer than you think — the rice really needs to turn golden brown, which takes a while.

Rotate the skillet or the rice every now and then so the rice is evenly crunchy and browned. Add more oil as needed — you should see the oil bubbling at the sides. When the rice is nearly ready, put a spoonful of butter on the tip of a knife and place it against the edge of the skillet. Drag the butter along the side of the skillet so it covers everything. Fry the rice for 1 minute more. This will make the underside extra crunchy and tasty.

Turn off the heat and carefully remove the rice from the skillet. You can do this by lifting it out using one or two spatulas, or loosen the sides of the rice with a spatula, invert a plate over the skillet and flip the skillet over quickly so the rice turns out onto the plate. Watch out for the hot oil. Serve the rice with the toppings of your choice: I like ginger mushrooms, Love Potion, crème fraîche and lemon zest.

(VARIATION): You can serve crispy rice with anything you like. The photo on the facing page shows it with leftover zesty mushrooms, Love Potion and crème fraîche, but I often have it very simply for lunch with a fried egg, chili oil and a combination of sliced green onions and fresh cilantro leaves.

Eggs are often my salvation when I just don't know what to cook. Eggs can be humble but also very luxurious. If I'm really at my wits' end, I'll just have scrambled egg cooked with tomato (for extra nutrients), on bread for dinner. Or I'll stir a scoop of sambal and some grated coconut into scrambled eggs for something spicy served over rice. Putting a perfectly boiled egg with a soft yolk on a dish immediately makes it chic and sexy. Or, try a spoonful of fish roe on scrambled eggs for a fabulous cozy weekend breakfast. As long as you always have a few eggs on hand, you can choose to go sexy or cozy at a moment's notice.

Eggs are often my salvation at times when I just don't know what to cook. Eggs can be humble but also very luxurious.

Iranian-Inspired Herbed Omelet with Spinach

This green omelet is entirely inspired by Iranian kuku sabzi, a thick omelet made with lots and lots of herbs. There are so many herbs you almost can't tell that there's egg in it! Kuku sabzi is hugely popular outside of Iran and it's no wonder: It's easy to make and the flavor is mind-blowing. I especially love the deliciously crispy edges. I have slightly adjusted the egg-to-herb ratio and added spinach, so it's a complete meal served with some tasty bread. I hope the popularity of Iranian cuisine continues to grow because it's my new obsession.

$6^2/_3$ cups (200 g) spinach

$^1/_3$ cup (15 g) chopped fresh dill

$^1/_3$ cup (15 g) chopped fresh basil

$^1/_3$ cup (15 g) chopped fresh cilantro leaves and tender stems

1 tsp ground cumin

$^1/_2$ tsp Aleppo pepper or hot pepper flakes (approx.)

Salt

3 eggs

Neutral oil for cooking

Bread for serving

Bring a saucepan of generously salted water to a boil. Add the spinach and blanch for 30 to 45 seconds, until wilted. Drain and place it in a strainer. Rinse under the tap with some cold water to cool it down a little. Drain again and then, using a clean tea towel or paper towel, squeeze as much moisture out of the spinach as possible. Coarsely chop the spinach and transfer to a bowl.

Add dill, basil, cilantro, ground cumin, $^1/_2$ tsp Aleppo pepper and a pinch of salt to the bowl. Whisk in the eggs. Heat a generous splash of neutral oil in a medium skillet over medium heat. Spread the egg mixture into the skillet. Cook the omelet for a few minutes, until browned and crispy around the edges and firm on the underside, rotating the omelet a little to ensure it cooks through evenly.

Using two spatulas, carefully flip over the entire omelet. (Fortunately, it'll still be tasty if it breaks — you could even turn it into three mini pancakes.) Heat the omelet on other side for a few minutes, until cooked through. Remove it from the pan and drain on plate lined with paper towels or on a wire rack. Sprinkle with a little more Aleppo pepper on it. Serve with your choice of bread. Pita or flatbread would be ideal but sourdough is good, too.

(LEFTOVERS): Three eggs are often just slightly too much for me, but this omelet makes a fantastic 4 p.m. snack. It's delicious cold or at room temperature. You can also double the recipe and take it to work the next day on a whole wheat bun.

Rice with Marinated Egg

Marinated eggs are the perfect snack to keep in your fridge and they take almost no time to prepare. If you're already going to the trouble of cooking one or two eggs, you might as well cook a few extra! Usually the thought of a cold boiled egg gives me the shivers, but I make an exception for marinated eggs. The eggs absorb all the flavors from the soy sauce and change color. There are countless ways to try this technique. Beet juice and some fresh dill would make pink eggs. This recipe is Korean-inspired and is fairly flexible. I just wing it and it's always delicious. Try adding some vinegar or a dollop of honey to the marinade or dilute the soy sauce with a little water. The best part is that you can pour the marinade liquid over any vegetable, from blanched spinach to edamame or broccoli, like I suggest here.

Bring water to a boil in a medium saucepan. Gently slide in the eggs and cook for 5 minutes, if you like soft yolks. Marinating the eggs in the next step will firm up the eggs a little, so if you usually cook a soft-boiled egg for 6 minutes, you should follow my directions.

Meanwhile, grab the smallest-possible airtight container that will fit the eggs. Combine the soy sauce, sesame oil and sugar in the container and stir until the sugar dissolves. Grate the garlic into the container and cut the green onion into thin rings. Add the green onion and sesame seeds to the container; stir to combine.

Using a slotted spoon, remove the eggs from the saucepan and shock them in a small bowl filled with ice water. Carefully peel the eggs and transfer them to the container with the sauce. The eggs may not be fully submerged, but that's okay. Marinate the eggs in the fridge for at least 4 hours, turning every now and then, but ideally all day or overnight. You can

Marinated eggs

2 eggs

3 tbsp (45 mL) soy sauce

1 tsp toasted sesame oil

1/2 tsp granulated sugar

1 small garlic clove

1 green onion

1 tsp toasted sesame seeds

The rest

1/2 cup (100 g) jasmine rice

7 oz (200 g) broccoli (about 2 1/4 cups chopped) or your chosen vegetable

(LEFTOVERS): I always cook a whole head of broccoli all at once — just make sure the water is generously salted so the broccoli has lots of flavor. I also like to cut it into smaller pieces and serve it with feta and chili oil on toast the next day. It's also handy to have broccoli available to stir into dishes, such as a curry, at the last moment for some extra veggies. Or, make a delicious salad with cooked beans.

keep them for up to a week, but I think they taste best if they're eaten within 1 to 4 days. They become firmer and saltier as time goes on.

Cook the rice as described on page 81 or according to package directions. Transfer to a bowl.

Bring a medium saucepan of salted water to a boil. Thinly slice the stem of the broccoli and cut the rest into large florets. Add the stem pieces to the saucepan and cook for 1 minute. Add the florets and cook until everything is tender. Drain and place on top of the cooked rice.

Cut one or two eggs in half, reserving marinade, and place on the rice. Spoon the sauce over everything; serve.

Za'atar Chips

1 whole wheat Lebanese flatbread, pita or leftover Flatbread (see page 37)

1 tbsp olive oil

2 tbsp za'atar

Preheat the oven to 350°F (180°C). Cut or tear the flatbread into pieces and place on a baking sheet. Drizzle with the olive oil, sprinkle with za'atar and spread out on the sheet. Bake for about 10 minutes, until golden brown and crispy. Lebanese flatbread is very thin and needs slightly less time than pita or homemade flatbread, so keep an eye on it. Pita and homemade flatbread need about 15 minutes.

Dill Scrambled Eggs with Za'atar Chips

For a long time, chives were my go-to herb on my weekend scrambled eggs, until a girlfriend turned me on to dill. Once I tried it, there was no going back. I've tried everything — dill mixed into the beaten eggs, frying the dill — but the very best way to eat it is to add a sprinkle of fresh dill over top of the eggs right before serving. I often eat this with toast for breakfast, but if you dress it up just a little bit more, it can absolutely be a complete dinner. I'm doubling down on dill here: There is fresh sprinkled on top and the dried in a dramatic sizzle of za'atar sauce drizzled over the eggs and veggies.

Sauce

1 tsp za'atar

1 tsp dried dill

2 tbsp finely chopped fresh dill

1½ tbsp olive oil

The rest

2 eggs

Salt

Olive oil for frying

1 serving of Za'atar Chips (see page 101)

3 tbsp (10 g) torn fresh dill leaves

For the sauce, combine the za'atar, dried dill and fresh dill in a heat-resistant bowl. Heat the olive oil in a saucepan over medium heat. Using a sprig of fresh dill, test whether the oil is hot enough (if so, it will sizzle immediately). Pour the hot oil over the ingredients in the bowl, stir and let stand while you make the rest of the dish.

Beat the eggs with a pinch of salt in a small bowl. Heat a few tablespoons of oil in a skillet over medium heat. Add the eggs and gently push them around until nearly cooked through. Remove from the heat; the eggs will continue to cook a little more. Stir and serve with the za'atar chips, sauce, fresh dill leaves and maybe some tomato and cucumber (see tip).

(LEFTOVERS): The za'atar sauce is also delicious over pasta or vegetables, or as a spread on bread with cottage cheese or feta.

(VEGETABLES): I often eat this for breakfast, but if I want some veggies for lunch or dinner, I'll just add some sliced cucumber and tomato. Scoop the sauce over top and you're done.

Çılbır with Spinach

Çılbır, the Turkish breakfast dish, is as simple and delicious as it is photogenic. Although it's traditionally made with poached eggs, I prefer soft-boiled eggs, especially since it's so much easier to make at home. Hard-boiled eggs also work well here. I add some cooked spinach on the side to round out the meal.

2 eggs

$^2/_3$ cup (150 g) plain Turkish or Greek yogurt

1 small garlic clove

Salt

$6^2/_3$ cups (200 g) spinach

2 tbsp butter

Aleppo pepper

Flaky sea salt

Whole wheat Flatbread (see page 37) or pita for serving

Bring a large saucepan of salted water to a boil.

Boil water in a medium saucepan. Add the eggs and cook for 5 minutes, or a bit longer if you prefer a firmer yolk.

Meanwhile, spoon the yogurt into a bowl and grate the garlic over top. Add a pinch of salt.

Add the spinach to the large saucepan and blanch for 30 to 45 seconds, until wilted. Drain and rinse under cold running water to stop the cooking process. Let the spinach drain in a strainer over the sink and, using a clean tea towel or paper towel, squeeze out as much liquid as possible.

Using a slotted spoon, remove the eggs from the saucepan and shock them in a small bowl filled with ice water. Spoon the garlicky yogurt onto a plate and spread it out with the back of a spoon. Cut the eggs in half and place them on the yogurt. Add the spinach.

Melt the butter in a small saucepan or skillet. Add Aleppo pepper to taste. Cook for a few seconds and then pour it over all the ingredients on the plate. Finish with a pinch of flaky sea salt and serve with flatbread or pita.

(VARIATIONS): I "çılbır" just about everything. By that I mean I'll eat some on garlicky yogurt with an Aleppo pepper butter drizzled over top. Think veggies, baked potatoes, fried tofu: I highly recommend you try it. You can also substitute the spinach in this recipe for other leafy greens, such as the Tuscan kale on page 123.

EAT YOUR VEGGIES

VEGGIES EAT Y

UR VEGGIES

R VEGGIES E

EGGIES EAT Y

UR VEGGIES

R VEGGIES E

EGGIES EAT Y

UR VEGGIES

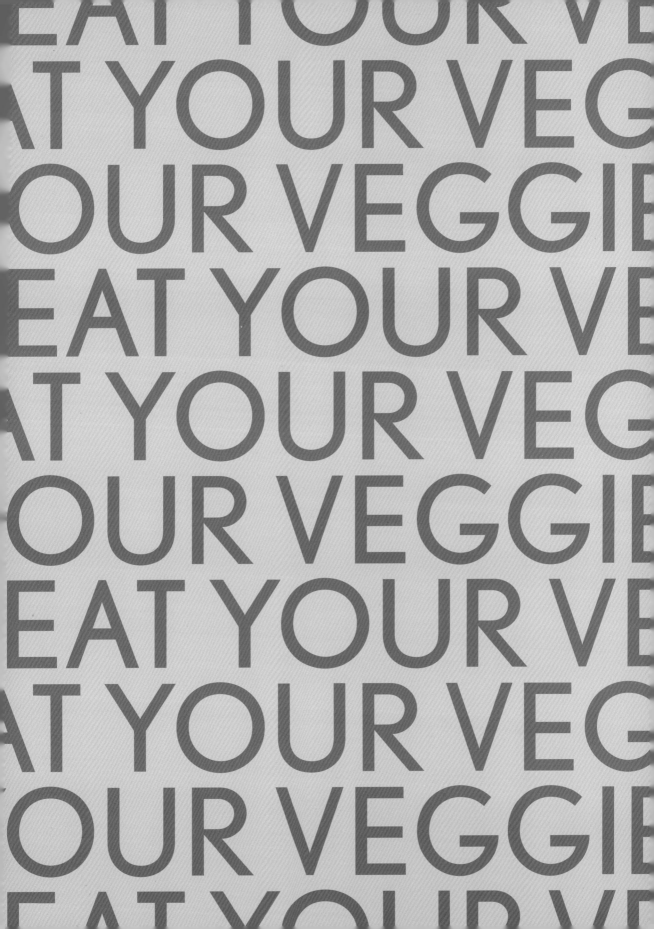

As I wrote earlier in this book, I think I have a different perspective than most people on the acceptable proportion of vegetable, protein and carbohydrates in any given meal. I don't think dinner always has to be complete. Sometimes if I post a noodle recipe on TikTok, someone will ask, "Where are the veggies?" Or, if I just eat grilled vegetables with egg, I get hit with: "That's too small, I'd eat a whole bag of chips afterwards." I respect you should take TikTok comments with a grain of salt, but the point of the story is that I think it's fine to play around a little with how you eat your veggies. This chapter will give you a few vegetable-forward meals you can fall back on and a few superfast side dishes, too.

This chapter will give you a few vegetable-forward meals you can fall back on.

Korean-Style Eggplant–Green Onion Pancake

I love Korean pancakes of all kinds, from green onion (pajeon) to seafood green onion (haemul pajeon) to vegetable (yachaejeon). Before I visited South Korea, I daydreamed about finding green onion pancakes — my favorite — at every street corner. I was slightly confused to discover that was not the case at all: Pajeon was most often served as a side dish at restaurants, not as street food.

So, I got my wish and ordered one with almost every meal. At home, I make a variation containing vegetables. If it's sufficiently filled, this pancake makes a fine dinner, in my books. For added protein, you could add some cubed tofu (firm or silken — it doesn't make much difference) to the batter.

(VARIATIONS): These pancakes are traditionally made with rice flour, which makes them so crunchy. However, you may have to go to an Asian grocery store to buy it, depending on the availability at your supermarket. So, I've substituted cornstarch here, which gives approximately the same effect. If you do have rice flour on hand, you can make the batter using $4\frac{1}{2}$ tbsp (40 g) white rice flour and the all-purpose flour.

Yachaejeon is a fantastic way to use all of your vegetables. It often contains grated carrot or zucchini or finely chopped cabbage or onion, but I've also made it with leftover roasted cauliflower or cooked broccoli.

---

5 oz (150 g) eggplant

Sunflower oil for frying

1 large green onion or 2 small

1 egg

$\frac{1}{3}$ cup (40 g) cornstarch

4 tbsp + 2 tsp (40 g) all-purpose flour

Salt

1 tbsp soy sauce

1 tbsp rice vinegar

optional for the dip: toasted sesame seeds, thinly sliced green onion, grated garlic, drizzle of toasted sesame oil

---

Cut the eggplant into matchsticks. Heat plenty of oil (the eggplant must be half submerged) in a medium skillet over medium heat. Cook the eggplant, stirring often, until browned and cooked through, about 5 to 10 minutes. The strips can be really nicely browned: When the eggplant is thinly sliced, it almost becomes slightly bacon-like.

Meanwhile, thinly slice the green onion into rings. Combine the sliced green onion, egg, cornstarch, flour, 3 tbsp + 1 tsp (50 mL) water and a pinch of salt in a bowl. Add the batter to the skillet with the eggplant. Increase the heat to high and cook the pancake on both sides until golden brown and crispy, about 5 minutes total. Drain on a wire rack, if you have one, or transfer to a plate lined with paper towel.

For the dip, combine the soy sauce, rice vinegar and any of the optional ingredients you like in a small bowl.

Cut the pancake into wedges and serve with the dip alongside.

Roasted Cauliflower with Za'atar

I make sure I always have cauliflower on hand for days when I don't feel like cooking but do want to eat a good amount of veg. Other than assembling the ingredients, the only thing you need to cook is the cauliflower. If you're too lazy to even cut up a cauliflower, buy one precut. Za'atar is so complex and flavorful that it magically changes your cauliflower into something delicious.

$1/2$ large cauliflower

Olive oil

Freshly ground black pepper

Salt

$2/3$ cup (150 g) labneh (see page 37), hummus (see page 37) or thick plain yogurt with a pinch of salt mixed in

---

2 tbsp za'atar

Whole wheat pita or Flatbread (see page 37)

Preheat the oven to 425°F (220°C).

Remove the leaves from the cauliflower and place them in a large bowl. Cut the cauliflower into medium florets. Add to the bowl with the leaves and combine with a generous dash of olive oil, pepper and salt. Spread out on a baking sheet and roast for 15 minutes. Reduce the temperature to 350°F (180°C) and roast for another 10 to 20 minutes, turning occasionally. Reducing the temperature ensures the cauliflower browns nicely on the outside but stays tender on the inside.

Spread the labneh on a plate with the back of a spoon. Add the cooked cauliflower florets and leaves over top. Finish with a drizzle of olive oil and the za'atar. Serve with pita or flatbread.

(LEFTOVER CAULIFLOWER): When I'm cooking for myself, I always roast the whole cauliflower and save the other half for later. It's delicious in creamy pasta (see page 123) or added to tomato sauce (see page 35), but also on a grilled sandwich (see page 52) or as part of a little plate (see page 62).

Eat Your Veggies

Harissa-Eggplant Caprese

I eat a caprese sandwich at least once a week and make sure to include a mozzarella ball on my weekly grocery list. Even when I'm working at my favorite café, nine times out of ten I order a caprese sandwich. One of my best friends has teased me about this for as long as I can remember because she thinks it's so basic, but I don't care. Try to get good buffalo mozzarella if you can because it makes a caprese really shine.

1 tbsp spicy harissa paste or rose harissa paste

3 tbsp (45 mL) olive oil (approx.)

1 garlic clove

Salt

Freshly ground black pepper

$\frac{1}{2}$ large eggplant or 1 small one

1 tomato

Small handful of fresh basil

Small handful of fresh chives

Drizzle of vinegar or freshly squeezed lemon juice

1 small fresh mozzarella cheese ball

Fried Bread (see page 49) for serving

Preheat the oven to 400°F (200°C).

Combine the harissa paste and olive oil in a medium bowl. Grate the garlic clove over top and season with salt and pepper. Cut the eggplant into $\frac{3}{4}$- by $1\frac{1}{4}$-inch (2 by 3 cm) pieces; add it to the harissa mixture and stir to combine. Spread the eggplant into a baking dish and roast for 30 to 40 minutes, turning occasionally, until completely soft and brown in some places. Remove the eggplant from the oven and let it cool to room temperature.

Meanwhile, cut the tomato into pieces. Season with salt to taste and let it stand for 10 minutes. Meanwhile, coarsely chop the basil. Cut the chives as finely as possible. Combine the tomato, basil, chives, eggplant and all the harissa oil from the baking dish on a plate or bowl. Add a tiny drizzle of vinegar and add more oil if necessary. Add salt to taste if needed. Tear the mozzarella into pieces and gently stir in to combine. Serve with toast on the side.

(VARIATIONS): This recipe can be made with any combination of herbs that you like. Basil does have the most caprese-like vibes, but dill, for example, will give it slightly more Middle Eastern flavors.

(HARISSA-EGGPLANT LEFTOVERS): Use any leftover eggplant on flatbread with labneh (see page 37) and dill. It is also delicious over rice, with a spoonful of thick plain yogurt and more herbs. Or, try it on toasted bread or in a grilled sandwich with tomato and mozzarella or another mild cheese.

(LEFTOVER HARISSA DRESSING): This is tasty on all roasted vegetables (cauliflower and green beans are two stars), as a salad dressing (with cucumber and little gem lettuce) or on crunchy roasted chickpeas or beans.

DAMN, STILL
NEED VEGGIES

It's so easy to make a quick pasta or a bowl of rice. I do love vegetables, but very often I don't feel like preparing another dish if the one I've already made doesn't contain veggies. And I've never understood the need to just throw vegetables into pasta sauce. I prefer to eat them separately. If you don't want to do more work but still want some vegetables, you can make something from page 119.

Tomatoes with Tahini Mayo

Coarsely chop a tomato and sprinkle with salt to taste. In a bowl, combine tahini and mayonnaise until it's your preferred consistency. I usually use three times more mayonnaise than tahini, but because tahini can vary in thickness, you should decide for yourself. If you use Japanese Kewpie mayonnaise, add a squeeze of lemon juice to the mixture. You may also want to dilute the sauce with a little bit of warm water to make it more runny. Drizzle the tahini mayo over the tomatoes and garnish with finely chopped chives.

(VARIATIONS): Tahini Mayo tastes great drizzled over most vegetables. Think seared broad beans, cooked green beans, or even iceberg lettuce prepared as a wedge salad. It's also good on grilled eggplant or with dill instead of chives.

Green Beans with Olives

Trim some green beans. Bring a saucepan of generously salted water to a boil. Cook the green beans for about 3 to 5 minutes, until crisp-tender and bright green. Meanwhile, finely chop a handful of Taggiasche or Kalamata olives. Drain the green beans and combine with the olives and a dash of olive oil. There is no need to add more salt because the olives are already salty.

(VARIATIONS): Try adding the olive mixture to blanched spinach or Tuscan kale, raw tomato, radicchio or Belgian endive.

Green or Napa Cabbage

Thinly slice some green or napa cabbage into the smallest-possible strips. Add to a bowl and toss with a squeeze of lemon juice, some salt and a dash of olive oil. Massage the dressing into the cabbage and eat immediately or let stand to soften the cabbage.

(VARIATIONS): Little gem, romaine lettuce or broccoli stems cut super thinly will also work here. It's also good with red cabbage; this does need to be marinated a little longer to wilt; otherwise, it stays hard. If you're serving it with an Asian dish, consider substituting lime juice for the lemon juice, and replace the olive oil with fish sauce (just don't add salt in that case).

Grated Carrot

Grate carrot (or buy pre-grated carrot) and mix with whatever you want! Mustard, olive oil, lemon, capers and parsley all work here, as does lemon juice, olive oil and salt, or olive oil and olives. You can also sauté grated carrot in oil with a pinch of salt. It takes very little time and changes the taste completely.

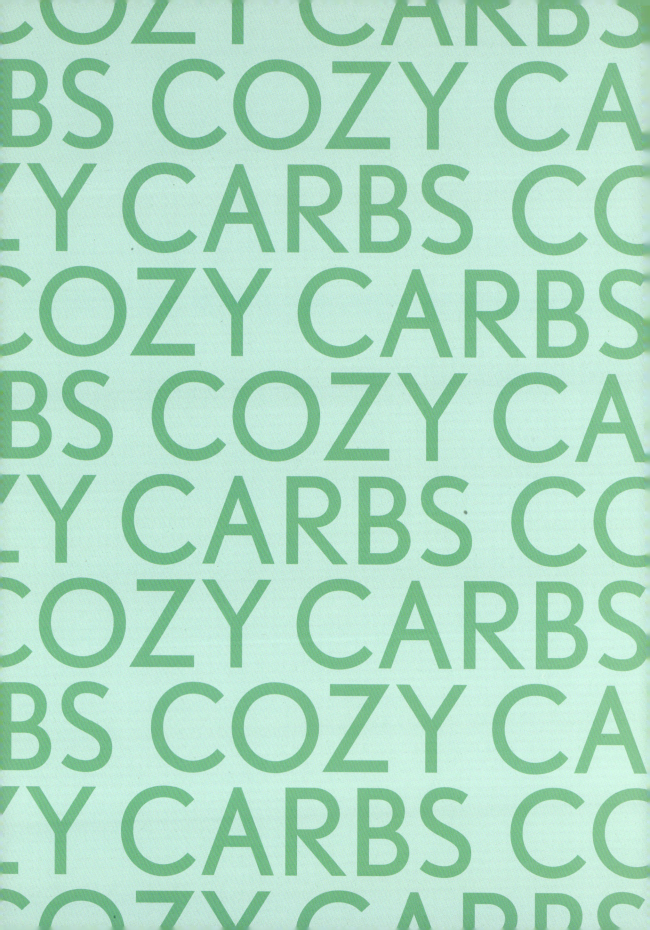

Buttery Pasta with Tuscan Kale

If I don't know what to eat in the winter months, I very often start by cooking kale in olive oil with lots of garlic. Once that's ready, I know with certainty there's a good meal ahead. It's delicious with, in and on everything (see tips). My absolute favorite recipe is this buttery pasta. It's the ultimate combination of comfy, creamy, zesty and fresh.

(VARIATIONS): By now I know a million variations on this pasta. I actually copied this recipe from my friend Yvette van Boven, who made it for me when I was visiting her and was sick as a dog. She added anchovies. I have a similar recipe in my noodle book where I use miso. You can also give it more depth by adding ground turmeric and coriander seeds as you cook the kale, and serving it with seed crisps (see page 130) over top.

When I make this pasta, I usually cook up the entire bunch of Tuscan kale and set some of it aside for later use, since sautéed kale with garlic is one of my favorite vegetables. (I really had to make an effort to use other vegetables in this book because I eat virtually nothing else in winter.) Use Tuscan kale to replace the spinach in the çılbır (see page 105), eat it on a grilled sandwich (see page 52) or add combine it other small snacks to make a little plate (see page 62). It's also tasty on rice with a marinated egg (see page 98) or as some additional veg for your rice with tuna bowl (see page 82). Spread some kale over a piece of toast with a fried egg and you have a fantastic lunch. Stir it into noodles, or eat it on toast with labneh (see page 37), feta or cottage cheese. I could go on and on . . .

5 oz (150 g) Tuscan kale, curly kale, green cabbage or spinach

3 garlic cloves

Olive oil for frying

Hot pepper flakes to taste

Salt

$3\frac{1}{2}$ oz (100 g) rigatoni or other pasta

2 tbsp butter

Parmesan cheese

Remove the Tuscan kale from the stems and coarsely cut into pieces (discard tough stems). Finely chop the garlic. Heat lots of olive oil in a large skillet over low heat and cook the kale, garlic, hot pepper flakes and a pinch of salt for 10 minutes, stirring often. The kale will already be tasty by now, but at this point I usually add a dash of water and let the whole thing simmer with the lid on, sometimes for 5 minutes but up to 20 minutes if I have the time. The kale will get darker and softer, so try out what works for you.

Meanwhile, boil a generously salted saucepan of water. Add the pasta and cook for 2 minutes less than it says on the package. Drain, reserving about 1 cup (250 mL) pasta cooking water. Add pasta, a little over $\frac{3}{4}$ cup (200 mL) reserved pasta water and butter to the kale in the pan. Cook over low heat, stirring until most of the liquid has evaporated and you get a nice glossy sauce. Add more pasta water as necessary. Serve sprinkled with Parmesan cheese.

Brothy Beans

Cooking one serving of beans is absurd. Though you could argue that cooking a big saucepan of beans is, in fact, not practical for one person. This might be true if you don't eat at home often, but my recipe gives you enough beans to make three to five different meals, depending on what you choose. Not to mention homemade beans are so much tastier than canned. I always initially eat my beans with the broth they're cooked in, hence "brothy beans."

I keep leftover beans in an airtight container in the fridge and stir them with abandon into salads and curries (see page 127) or mash them on toast.

(VARIATIONS): These are my standard ingredients for brothy beans, but please use what you want. You could sauté onion and garlic in olive oil first before adding the beans. You can also add fresh herbs or other spices. Be careful with the latter, since it's hard to fish out whole peppercorns or coriander seeds, for example, and they aren't so tasty. Or, put them in a tea infuser or spice bag before adding to the saucepan. I cook chickpeas the same way; they just need a bit more time, sometimes up to 2 hours.

An easy and classic way of making this dish is to sauté or blanch Tuscan kale, spinach or another leafy green and stir it into the beans. This is my favorite way to eat it, but also experiment with radicchio, leek or peas in spring. Or, I serve it with a crunchy lettuce or tomato salad.

Brothy beans

1½ cups (300 g) dried beans (cannellini/white kidney, black-eyed peas, lima, pinto, Romano, whatever you like)

1 piece of Parmesan cheese rind or kombu

3 dried chile peppers

1 small onion or shallot

A few garlic cloves

2 bay leaves

Dash of olive oil

Pinch of dried thyme or oregano (really just a little, for a background flavor)

Salt

Serve with

An extra dash of olive oil or chili oil

Bread or toast

In the morning or the night before, place the beans in a bowl with plenty of cold water. Soak at room temperature for at least 8 hours.

Drain the beans and place them in a large saucepan with enough water to cover them by about ½ inch (1 cm). Add the Parmesan cheese rind, chile peppers, onion, garlic, bay leaves, olive oil, dried thyme and some salt; bring to a boil over high heat. Reduce the heat to low and let the beans simmer gently until tender, adding more water as necessary. I usually want some liquid in the saucepan by the end of the cooking process for my one serving of brothy beans, but if the beans are no longer submerged after a while, that's okay. They do, however, need enough water to cook in, though.

How much time the beans need to cook depends on the type. Small beans may be done after just 30 minutes; sometimes you need 1 hour. Start tasting after 30 minutes and cook until tender enough for your liking. Discard Parmesan cheese rind, dried chiles, onion, bay leaves and garlic. Spoon the rest of the beans into an airtight container and refrigerate for later. Serve with a dash of olive oil or chili oil and bread alongside for dipping.

Cozy Carbs

BEANY IDEAS FOR THE REST OF THE WEEK

Use leftover Brothy Beans in so many different ways.

Beans with Vinaigrette

This is the easiest way of all. Combine the cooked beans, one or more vegetables and vinaigrette (see page 141) in a bowl. Slightly mash everything together. Serve on bread. It's delicious with lots of herbs on top, if you have them. The vegetables can be precooked, possibly leftovers, but raw veg such as radicchio, Belgian endive or little gem lettuce will also work.

Fried Oyster Mushrooms

Sauté oyster mushrooms in a dash of olive oil in a skillet over high heat, until golden brown. Add spinach, rapini or another soft green vegetable. Add the cooked beans, stir and heat until warmed through. Serve with an extra dash of olive oil, lemon zest, a boiled egg and Fried Bread alongside (see page 49).

Indian-ish Beans

Sauté 1 small onion, 2 garlic cloves and a 1¼-inch (3 cm) piece of fresh gingerroot (all finely chopped) in neutral oil or

ghee. Add 1 teaspoon of ground cumin, 1 teaspoon of ground turmeric and 1 teaspoon of garam masala and cook until fragrant. Add the cooked beans and $\frac{2}{3}$ cup (150 mL) coconut milk or bean broth if you still have some left. Stir until the beans are warmed through. Sprinkle lots of finely chopped fresh cilantro over top. Shallot crisps are also a delicious option as a garnish if you have some left (see page 144). Serve with rice or Flatbread (see page 37).

Italian Bean Soup

Sauté 1 small onion and 2 garlic cloves (both finely chopped) in a saucepan in olive oil. Add Tuscan kale (finely chopped) and tomato (diced); cook for 5 minutes. Pour in your favorite broth (which could be your bean broth!) and bring to a boil. Add cooked small orecchiette or other small pasta and cooked beans; stir. Serve with finely chopped parsley sprinkled over top and Fried Bread (see page 49) on the side.

Beans on Toast

Mash the cooked beans with a fork so that half of the beans are mashed and some are still whole. Combine with a dash of olive oil and fresh herbs and spread onto toast.

Takeout Leftovers

If you've ordered Indian, Thai or something in a curry-like sauce, you often get more sauce than you need. Keep the sauce and stir in some cooked beans the next day. Ordering in is expensive and this lets you enjoy takeout for another day.

Pasta with Cherry Tomatoes, Anchovy and Garlic-Pistachio Crisps

Pasta with tomato sauce may be the ultimate quick meal. In the winter, I often make a super-easy sauce by combining canned tomatoes, garlic, anchovies and butter in a small baking dish. Slide it into the oven for 30 minutes, mash with a fork and you have the easiest tomato sauce ever. I usually make this sauce with fresh tomatoes during the sunnier months, still with anchovies, butter and garlic, but just a little different.

(VARIATIONS): If you'd prefer a vegan meal, you can omit the anchovies. The garlic-pistachio crisps are tasty enough to carry the pasta. It's delicious with fresh basil as well if you have some.

(LEFTOVER ANCHOVIES): I always buy jarred anchovies because they can keep in the fridge longer than an opened can. That being said, canned anchovies freeze surprisingly well. If you'd rather use a whole jar or can of anchovies at once, make anchovy butter. Finely chop the anchovies and stir them into softened butter. Bonus points for whipping the butter with a mixer. This butter is best kept in the fridge. You'll finish it in no time. Put it on an egg with mayonnaise, tomato toast or buttered bread, or add it to the pasta with Tuscan kale (see page 123).

| 2 garlic cloves |
| Handful of raw shelled pistachios |
| Olive oil for frying |
| Flaky sea salt |
| 3½ oz (100 g) spaghetti |
| 1 cup (150 g) cherry tomatoes |
| 2 tbsp butter |
| 3 anchovy fillets |
| Freshly ground black pepper |

Finely chop the garlic. Coarsely chop the pistachios. Heat a few tablespoons of olive oil over low heat in a medium skillet. Add the garlic and cook for a few minutes, stirring constantly, until golden brown and crunchy. (Make sure to keep the heat low and continue stirring or else the garlic will burn!) Once the garlic is slightly browned (it will keep cooking outside the pan), drain through a fine-mesh sieve set over a heatproof bowl to collect the oil. Transfer the garlic crisps to a plate lined with paper towel.

Pour the garlic oil back into the skillet and heat over low heat. Add the chopped pistachios and cook for a few minutes, stirring constantly, until golden brown. Add a bit more oil, if necessary, although the nuts don't need very much fat. They are already fatty. Add the browned pistachios, reserving the skillet, to the garlic on the paper towel, combine with a spoon and add salt to taste.

Bring a saucepan of generously salted water to a boil and cook the spaghetti according to the package directions.

Meanwhile, halve the cherry tomatoes. Melt the butter in a medium or large skillet over low heat. Add the anchovies and cook, stirring, until the anchovies have disintegrated. Add the tomatoes and a little bit of black pepper; cook for a few minutes, until softened. Drain the pasta, reserving a few tablespoons of cooking water. Add pasta and reserved water to the skillet; stir to combine. Spoon onto a plate and serve topped with the garlic-pistachio crisps.

Orzo with Cauliflower, Cashew Cream and Seed Crisps

I'd always pigeonholed cashew cream as a fit girl thing, so I'd never eaten it — until recently. I discovered that it's just wildly delicious, which makes sense because, when blended, cashews are fatty and creamy. Add a squeeze of lemon juice to blended cashews and it almost tastes like a crème fraîche–based pasta sauce, except entirely vegan. You can serve this sauce over most pastas, but I really like the mouth feel of orzo. Using small pasta almost gives a mac and cheese feel, but in an elegant, grown-up way.

7 tbsp (50 g) raw cashews

1 tbsp nigella seeds or black sesame seeds

1 tbsp coriander seeds

2 tbsp raw sesame seeds

Olive oil for frying

Flaky sea salt

¼ cauliflower

2 garlic cloves

½ cup + 1 tbsp (100 g) orzo

Juice of ½ lemon

Handful of chopped fresh dill leaves

You will find the recipe on page 133.

(LEFTOVER CAULIFLOWER): This pasta is the perfect way to use up leftover roasted cauliflower (see page 112). If you are using precooked cauliflower, skip the pan-frying step in this recipe. Sauté some garlic in a skillet, add the roasted cauliflower and heat until warmed through. Proceed with the rest of the recipe as directed.

(LEFTOVER NIGELLA SEEDS): If you don't have nigella seeds at home, you can omit them or replace them with black sesame seeds, but I do suggest you consider adding them to your pantry. They have a wonderfully distinct smoky flavor that is delicious in Flatbread (see page 37), dilly pancakes (see page 69) or the Tuscan kale pasta (see page 123) variation with ground turmeric.

(LEFTOVER SEED CRISPS): Freshly cooked seed crisps taste the best and require little effort. That being said, you could also make a whole bunch at once and sprinkle them on everything. These seed crisps would also be tasty over top the Harissa-Eggplant Caprese (see page 115) or dill scrambled eggs (see page 103). Or sprinkle them over a fried egg and drizzle with some quick chili oil (see page 86).

Set a couple of tablespoons of cashews aside for the crisps and soak the rest in a bowl of cold water. This doesn't need to be for long — just while you're preparing the other ingredients.

Coarsely chop the reserved cashews. Add the reserved cashews, nigella seeds, coriander seeds, sesame seeds and 1 tablespoon of olive oil to a small skillet; cook for a few minutes on low heat, stirring, until the nuts and the sesame seeds turn golden brown. This really can't be rushed, so make sure the heat is not too high and keep stirring. Making crisps requires patience. Drain the crisps on a plate lined with paper towel and sprinkle with flaky sea salt.

Cut the cauliflower into small florets. Heat a good dash of olive oil in a large shallow saucepan or skillet and cook the cauliflower over high heat for about 10 minutes, stirring often, until golden brown. Meanwhile, finely chop the garlic. A couple minutes just before the cauliflower is finished cooking, add garlic to the saucepan. Remove from the heat.

Now cook the orzo in a saucepan of generously salted water for 2 minutes less than it says on the package. You could also time things so the orzo is ready at the same time as the cauliflower, but orzo is very small, so it cooks quickly, which is why I prefer playing it safe. Drain the orzo, reserving 1 cup (250 mL) cooking water.

Purée the soaked cashews in about $^2/_3$ to $^3/_4$ cup (150 to 175 mL) of the pasta cooking water in a tall cup using an immersion blender. Season to taste with lemon juice and salt.

Add the cashew cream and orzo to the cauliflower in the skillet. Cook over medium heat, stirring constantly, until the orzo is tender and most of the liquid has been absorbed. Orzo absorbs water quickly, so you can also add a bit of the reserved pasta cooking water to achieve the right creaminess. It will continue to thicken off the heat, so you'll want it on the runnier side. Ladle the orzo into a deep plate and garnish with the seed crisps. Garnish with chopped dill.

DINING OUT ALONE

This is a cookbook, but sometimes you want to dine out by yourself, too. I have to admit I don't do it very often, except when I travel. Luckily for you I've traveled a lot, so I still have some tips for how to eat a successful restaurant dinner on your own.

Not every city makes it easy. It's always disappointing for me to compare the Netherlands to some places abroad. For example, it's much more common to go out to eat alone in New York or London; therefore, it's more inviting to do so. Many restaurants in those cities have great bars or just good places to sit by yourself, often by a window so you can look outside during your meal. Restaurants in many Asian countries are also set up for one, and don't require an awkward song and dance of removing the second place setting once you announce you'll be alone. There is universal room for improvement, but here are some of my general tips, no matter where you are.

No Place for One? Call!

I regularly find that I'm unable to make a reservation just for one in many online booking systems. If reserving a table is only possible for two or more, call the restaurant. Sometimes there are restrictions online, but an actual person can find you a spot. Sometimes this is not the case, but then at least you know for sure. Many restaurants also do walk-ins only for one at the bar.

Big Table

Some restaurants have big communal tables, which I love. This is often the case at cafés and restaurant-cafés where you'll be eating among laptop users. Maybe you'll feel more at ease around other solo guests. Some fancier restaurants now also have communal tables where you can eat a multicourse meal. At Raw in Taipei, for example, you don't get your own table unless there are at least two diners, but you can sit down at a communal table to enjoy your fancy meal.

Provide Entertainment

I like having lunch or a coffee with a newspaper; however, the newspaper itself takes up a fair amount of space so it's not great to bring when you want to eat a larger meal. My e-reader solves this problem. It's smaller than a book and can always fit somewhere on the table. Or, you can just look at your phone or be alone with your thoughts, of course. Everything is possible! It's just helpful to think ahead about what you'll be doing between courses. You could also ask the server to leave the menu with you so you can pretend to be reading it attentively even if you ordered already.

Ordering

Okay, so you're at the restaurant and you've figured out some entertainment to help pass the time. Now on to the food. When I'm traveling alone, I'm very food focused and I like to order multiple dishes. After all, you're often only there once! One of my tricks is to order multiple appetizers or side dishes, so you can try more things without filling up as quickly. Or, order things that will keep for the next day, so you can take

You Are Not Sad

Sometimes people think that everyone is staring at them when they dine alone and that is somehow sad. Are you only here because you couldn't convince anyone to go to a restaurant with you? Forget that. If you're brave enough to dine out alone, you're cooler than everyone else. In fact, I always feel very independent and tough. If people stare a little too long at you, it's probably because they're jealous that you find yourself such good company. Bon appétit.

S POTATOES
TATOES POTA
POTATOES PO
S POTATOES
TATOES POTA
POTATOES PO
S POTATOES
TATOES POTA
POTATOES PO
S POTATOES

POTATOES POTA
TOES POTATO
TATOES POTA
POTATOES PO
TOES POTATO
TATOES POTA
POTATOES PO
TOES POTATO
TATOES POTA
POTATOES PO

I love potatoes and, when I eat them, I eat them all week long. I buy a couple pounds of baby potatoes or big crumbly ones from my grocer on the weekend. If you have a good fruit and vegetable market or farmers' market in your area, go there. It might be a bit more expensive than the supermarket, but the taste difference is huge. Ever since I've started buying good-quality potatoes, I find I don't like the supermarket variety at all. (Buying most vegetables at the supermarket is perfectly fine.) I always cook the whole batch at once and eat potatoes different ways throughout the week.

This chapter has a few recipes for potato salad, but if you want something quicker, stir some leftover green herb mash (see page 61) into your spuds. Leftover boiled potatoes are also a delicious shortcut to a speedy meal. They're also tasty as a snack with a dollop of mayo and a caper on top.

I love potatoes and, when I eat them, I eat them all week long.

Dill-Caper Potato Salad

This potato salad is a great starting point that you can take in many different directions, depending on the season and how much you feel like cooking. It's the perfect foundation for a little plate (see page 62) if you add a boiled egg and some tomato. Or, you can stir in cooked green beans and eat it with a dollop of crème fraîche or labneh (see page 37) and some lemon zest. Other tasty additions include leftover roasted cauliflower (see page 112), harissa eggplant (see page 115) or Tuscan kale (see page 123), perhaps topped with seed crisps (see page 130).

7 oz (200 g) little potatoes

1 small shallot

1 small garlic clove

1 tbsp honey

1 tsp Dijon mustard

Juice of $\frac{1}{2}$ lemon

Salt

Freshly ground black pepper

$\frac{1}{3}$ cup (75 mL) olive oil

2 tbsp capers

$\frac{1}{3}$ cup (15 g) chopped fresh dill leaves

Heaping spoonful of crème fraîche

Place the little potatoes in a saucepan of generously salted water and bring to a boil. Cook the potatoes for 12 to 15 minutes or until tender.

Chop the shallot as finely as possible. Add the shallot to a large bowl. Grate the garlic and add it to the bowl along with the honey, mustard and lemon juice. Season to taste with salt and pepper; whisk until the honey dissolves. Slowly pour the olive oil into the bowl, whisking constantly, until combined. You will have a thick vinaigrette.

Drain the potatoes and let them cool for a bit in the strainer. Pinch the skin of each potato gently so the skin breaks a little, which will allow for better absorption of the vinaigrette.

Finely chop the capers. Add the capers, potatoes, dill and a few tablespoons of vinaigrette. The hotter the potatoes, the more vinaigrette they'll absorb, so how much you need depends a bit on the temperature. I usually make this with leftover little potatoes, so cold or at room temperature. Serve with a spoonful of crème fraîche.

(VINAIGRETTE FOR THE WHOLE WEEK): It's possible to make vinaigrette for one person, but I never do. You'll end up wasting ingredients and I find vinaigrette always comes in handy, anyways. If you leave the garlic out until just before you use it, the vinaigrette will keep for up to two weeks. It's always good for a quick salad or for mixing into vegetables. Store it in the fridge and you'll have enough for 3 or 4 servings.

Tofu Crème with Roasted Potatoes and Shallot Crisps

I like roasted potatoes best when they're big and crumbly, not little, because the big ones maximize the extra-crispy-exterior-to-tender-interior ratio. I often make roasted potatoes from leftover boiled potatoes I've prepared earlier in the week. Sometimes I find boiling and roasting at one time too much work, but if they're pre-boiled, the roasting step is a walk in the park. I'll often eat roasted potatoes with creamed spinach, vegetarian sausage or vegan fish sticks, but with a tiny bit more effort you can make something really delicious. Try it with a fresh salad, such as tomato or the carrot salad on page 119, or any leftover vegetables you may have.

7 oz (200 g) russet potato (about 1 medium)

Olive oil for frying

Salt

1 large shallot

2 garlic cloves

3 tbsp + 1 tsp (50 mL) sunflower oil

Flaky sea salt

Lots of fresh herbs, ideally a mix (dill, parsley, cilantro, basil or chives)

$2/3$ cup (150 g) Tofu Crème (see page 37), labneh (see page 37) or plain Greek yogurt

Freshly ground black pepper

1 tbsp vinegar (any type)

(LEFTOVER CRISPS): I actually never make crisps using just one shallot because leftover shallot crisps taste good on everything. I usually cut up three shallots and like five garlic cloves and fry them all at the same time. However, don't crowd the skillet with too many shallots or they won't become crunchy. The crisps will keep for at least a week in an airtight container at room temperature, but really I'd say it's longer. They'll soften after a while but they still taste great. Let the shallots cool before you store them; otherwise, they'll steam up the container and go limp.

Preheat the oven to 400°F (200°C).

Peel the potato and cut it into about 1¹/₂-inch (4 cm) pieces. Place in a saucepan of generously salted water. Bring to a boil over high heat and cook the potatoes for 12 to 15 minutes, until tender.

Drain the potatoes. Place them on a baking sheet and combine with a generous dash of olive oil. Sprinkle the potatoes with salt and spread out on the baking sheet. Roast in the preheated oven for 40 minutes, turning occasionally so that the potatoes cook evenly, until well browned. You can also fry the potatoes in a skillet, but I like to fry the shallot crisps while the potatoes are cooking.

Cut the shallot in half lengthwise, then cut each half lengthwise into thin slices. Thinly slice the garlic. Heat the sunflower oil in a skillet over medium heat. Add the garlic and shallot; cook, stirring constantly, for about 8 minutes, until golden brown and crunchy. Make sure the heat isn't too high or everything will burn. Making crisps requires a lot of love and attention. Drain the crisps, reserving oil, and place them on a plate lined with paper towel. Season with a pinch of flaky sea salt.

Finely chop the herbs. In a tall cup using an immersion blender, combine the herbs and Tofu Crème until smooth. Remove the potatoes from the oven. Sprinkle with a few good twists of black pepper and the vinegar. Taste and add more flaky sea salt if needed. Spread the tofu-herb mixture on a plate using the back of a spoon. Place the potatoes over top. Garnish with the shallot crisps and serve.

Sambal Matah Potatoes

Sambal matah is Balinese sambal that may not entirely match your idea of sambal, the spicy Indonesian red pepper paste. This version is a fresh "loose" sauce comprised of shallots, chile peppers and lime. It's delicious with grilled fish or meat or really anything else that could benefit from something zesty. It is usually made with wild lime leaves, which can be found at Asian grocery stores. I have omitted them from the recipe, since they can be difficult to find, but if you have them, please include them and leave out the lime zest. Just make sure to finely chop the lime leaves before adding them to the sambal. Regardless of whether or not you include the lime leaves, it's a delicious dressing for potatoes or vegetables. It's particularly good spooned over roasted potatoes.

7 oz (200 g) little potatoes
1 egg
7 oz (200 g) broccolini
Olive oil
Salt
2 small shallots
1 garlic clove
1/2-inch (1 cm) piece of fresh gingerroot
1 red chile pepper
2 tbsp sunflower oil
1 lime (preferably organic)
Handful of small tomatoes on the vine

Preheat the oven to 400°F (200°C).

Place the little potatoes in a saucepan of generously salted water and bring to a boil over high heat. As soon as the water is boiling, add the egg, cook for 5 minutes and remove with a slotted spoon. Shock it under cold running water to stop the cooking process. Continue to cook the potatoes for another 7 to 15 minutes, until tender.

Meanwhile, combine the broccolini, a few tablespoons of olive oil and a pinch of salt in a baking dish. Bake in the preheated oven for 15 minutes.

For the sambal matah, cut the shallots into small pieces. Mince the garlic, ginger and red chile pepper into the smallest possible pieces. You're eating the ingredients virtually raw, so it's not tasty to bite into big pieces. Put the shallots, garlic, ginger and chile pepper in a heatproof bowl. Heat the sunflower oil in a small saucepan over medium heat. Once the oil is hot, pour it over the ingredients in the bowl. Zest the lime over the bowl and add a squeeze of lime juice. Taste and add salt as needed.

Peel the boiled egg. Drain the potatoes and let them cool a little in a bowl. Quarter the tomatoes and combine with the potatoes and most of the sambal matah. Arrange the salad on a plate and top with the broccolini and the boiled egg. Scoop some more sambal matah over the broccolini and serve.

PARTY OF ONE
OF ONE PARTY
F ONE PARTY
PARTY OF ON
OF ONE PAR
F ONE PARTY
PARTY OF ON
OF ONE PAR
F ONE PARTY
PARTY OF ON

For the past few years, I've celebrated New Year's Eve on my own. I can't recommend it enough. I have zero FOMO because I've never been to a New Year's Eve party that I've actually enjoyed, except one at the height of COVID when my party consisted of me and one couple. I generally can't stay awake until midnight, so we ordered a whole lot of Chinese food, had champagne at ten and I was biking home moments later. It was perfect. When parties started happening again in the years that followed, I chose to have a nice evening at home instead.

It feels a little like having a Monday off when everyone else is working. I get to have a whole evening to myself while everyone else is partying in sequins. That being said, I want to still do something special, so I'll start thinking up the perfect meal weeks in advance. Even though I'm 100 percent sure I'm having a better time at home than at any party ever, sometimes you can still get down during the holidays. The Christmas markets and all the lights can almost trick you into thinking you have to go out even if you really don't feel like it.

Spending holidays on your own is difficult. I enjoy it immensely around New Year's Eve, but it's quite tricky for the rest of December. Mariah Carey blares from speakers and people talk about how much they love Christmas. It's a lot if you're really not feeling it, for whatever reason. You deserve to treat yourself during the holidays, although this applies to days when you have other things to celebrate — a promotion, book contract, tickets to Taylor Swift.

If you want to go all out with a three-course meal and wine pairings, be my guest. Generally, you can mix and match all the recipes in this book or another book. However, the two recipes in this chapter are my go-to holiday meals when I want to show myself some love and remind myself that I deserve the best.

Generally, you can mix and match all the recipes in this book or another book.

Rice Bowl with Marinated Fish Roe

Fish roe makes everything luxurious. It's exactly what you need to make an evening feel special without too much effort. They taste great spooned over scrambled eggs. Or, combine sour cream with chives, sprinkle with fish roe and serve with plain ripple chips for dipping. However, the perfect meal to eat on the couch for a solo party night is a rice bowl topped with fish roe.

1 tbsp soy sauce

$1/2$ tsp honey

$3^1/_2$ oz (100 g) salmon roe or trout roe

$1/2$ cup (100 grams) short-grain (sushi) rice

Combine the soy sauce and honey in a bowl; stir until the honey dissolves. Combine the fish roe with the soy sauce mixture and let stand in the fridge at least 4 hours before eating.

When you're ready for your festive dinner, cook the rice as described on page 81 or according to the package directions.

Spoon the marinated roe over the rice and serve.

(VARIATION): This recipe is inspired by Japanese ikura don. When I make ikura don, I marinate the roe in soy sauce, mirin and sake. However, you may have to go to a well-stocked grocery store, Asian supermarket and/or liquor store to buy these ingredients. Since I didn't include them in the Capsule Kitchen (see page 22), I modified the above recipe. You might feel okay about getting these ingredients, since you're having a party night anyways. If that's the case, omit the honey and add 1 teaspoon of mirin and 1 teaspoon of sake.

Cheese for One

This is not so much a recipe as it is a tribute to the humble cheese board. I almost never buy fancy cheeses for entertaining because I never finish them in one go. If I buy multiple cheeses, I often end up throwing them away because they go bad sooner than I can eat them. I'm just not a cocktail-hour person when the cheese usually comes out. My solution: Buying one piece of very tasty cheese, crackers or a good baguette, and a bunch of grapes. That's it.

In any case, I don't understand why a specific combination of cheeses should be served together. I choose what I feel like eating. If you're of the opinion that it's not a party until there are different cheeses on the board, that's fine, too, of course. Go to a good cheese store and get two to three small pieces, so you get a few bites of everything. Add a nice drink and your festive evening is complete.

Drinking for One

I never drink alcohol at home, but a nice drink can help create party vibes. That's why I always have nonalcoholic beer on hand at home as well as kombucha, seltzer or — my favorite — San Pellegrino Aranciata Rossa. There are increasingly more great nonalcoholic options popping up every day and stores that sell half bottles of wine, which are perfect for solo drinkers.

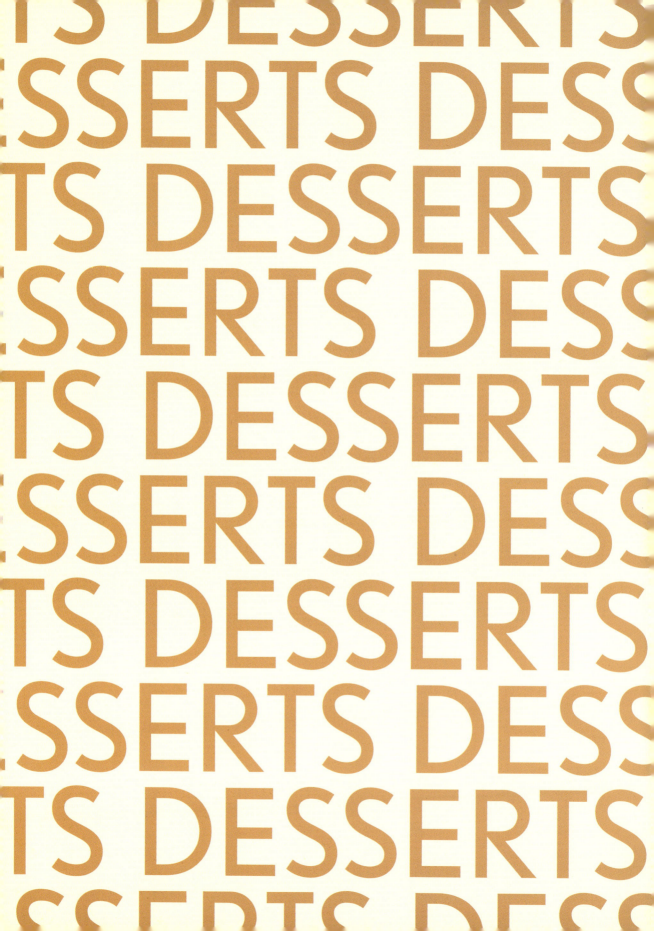

DESSERTS
ERTS DESSER
DESSERTS DE
ERTS DESSE
DESSERTS DE
ERTS DESSE
DESSERTS DE
ERTS DESSER
DESSERTS DE
ERTS DESSE

Baking is fun, but I always like to have at least one supermarket dessert on hand. If you only want a little dessert once or twice a week, it can be difficult to make sweet treats at home. Cookies become chewy after a few days; chocolate can haunt you, too, even from behind a closed door. Supermarkets have many perfect single-serving desserts and it'd be a shame not to take advantage of them. No matter how often I eat them, it always feels like a treat.

My favorites are: rice pudding (any brand), chocolate pudding with whipped cream on top, pistachio yogurt with almonds, and crème brûlée. If I'm in a luxurious mood or not feeling great, I occasionally buy a box of chocolate. I immediately feel posh, especially when I go to pick one out after dinner, like a present.

Supermarkets have many perfect single-serving desserts and it'd be a shame not to take advantage of them.

Boterkoek (Dutch Butter Pie)

This dessert tastes like something between a cake and a shortbread. I've given two versions here: one that uses dairy and one that is plant-based. The pie has a beautiful, shiny top layer because it's normally brushed with egg. A whole egg, however, is too much for such a small pic, so I went in search of a more user-friendly alternative. I discovered that you could get the same gloss using a combination of milk (or plant-based milk) and olive oil. Once I'd gotten that far, I figured I might as well try it with plant-based butter, too, and it turned out great. You can use dairy butter, of course: I've tested both versions and guess what? They're delectable.

The only downside to this recipe is that it tastes best if you let it cool for at least 3 hours, but preferably overnight. If you try it sooner, you might think you haven't made the recipe properly, because it doesn't get the right texture until it's cooled for a good long time. It's not a quick dessert to satisfy a post-dinner sugar craving.

(VARIATIONS): The pie also tastes great with either minced rosemary, minced wild lime leaves or lemon zest mixed into the dough.

$\frac{1}{4}$ cup (50 g) light brown sugar

3 tbsp + 1 tsp (50 g) butter or plant-based butter, at room temperature

7 tbsp (60 g) all-purpose flour

Salt

1 tbsp olive oil

1 tsp milk or plant-based milk

You will need

A small pie plate, 4 to 5 inches (10 to 12.5 cm) in diameter (such as an aluminum one or a springform pan)

Pastry brush

Preheat the oven to 350°F (180°C).

In a bowl, using your hands, combine the brown sugar, butter, flour and a pinch of salt just until it forms a dough. Do not over-knead the dough — if you have lots of pieces sticking together, you'll be fine. If you knead the dough for longer, the pie will be tough later. Press the dough into the pie plate. Drag a fork along the top to make a crisscross pattern.

In a small bowl, whisk together the olive oil and milk. Brush the mixture onto the pie. The pattern will be more visible on the pie if you put it in the fridge for 30 minutes first, but if you don't have the time, it's fine.

Bake in the preheated oven for 15 minutes or until the top is golden brown. Let it cool completely, preferably for at least 3 hours, before serving.

Quick Berry Crumble with Sesame Seeds

Crumble was my favorite dessert back when I was a student. My housemate and I used to shoot each other a certain look after dinner and we'd know it was crumble time. We always kept a bag of frozen fruit on hand for this purpose and then we'd whip up this dessert a few times a week, preferably with a scoop of vanilla ice cream. You can make this crumble in a ramekin or bake the crumbs separately, spreading them out on a baking sheet lined with parchment paper (following the recipe instructions). Sprinkle the crumbs on vanilla ice cream or fruit that has briefly been warmed in a pan. Sliced peaches are also a very good choice here.

(VARIATIONS): There are endless variations of this dessert. Apple crumble remains one of the most delicious things in the world, with a pinch of cinnamon or cardamom, for example. Try it using one of the fun berry blends from the frozen section of the supermarket. If you don't have a freezer, keep any leftover frozen fruit in the fridge and serve it on yogurt the next morning or mix it into a smoothie.

Topping

2½ tbsp (20 g) all-purpose flour

1 tbsp granulated sugar

2 tsp raw sesame seeds (perhaps a mix of black and white)

2 tbsp (30 g) butter

Pinch of salt

Fruit

¾ cup (120 g) frozen or fresh blueberries or other fruit

1 tbsp granulated sugar

1 tsp cornstarch

Grated zest and juice of ½ lemon (preferably organic)

1 scoop of vanilla ice cream (optional)

You will need

Large ramekin or ovenproof bowl

Preheat the oven to 350°F (180°C).

Combine the flour, sugar, sesame seeds, butter and salt in a medium bowl with your fingers just until crumbs form. Don't mix for too long or it will become sticky.

In another medium bowl, combine the blueberries, sugar, cornstarch and the lemon zest and juice. Spoon the blueberry mixture into a ramekin and spread the topping over it. Bake for 20 to 25 minutes, until the blueberries are bubbling and the topping is golden brown. Let it cool slightly and serve, perhaps with a scoop of ice cream over top.

Emoji Cookies

These cookies are perfect for when you want something sweet after dinner but don't feel like walking to the grocery store (assuming you have the ingredients at home). Cookie dough often needs to be refrigerated for a period of time, but this dough can be baked right away. Just 10 minutes in the oven and they're ready to eat.

I have to be honest: I didn't do much work for this recipe. I was staying with my friend Yvette van Boven in Ireland and she got so excited when I told her that I still needed a cookie recipe for my book. Before I knew it, she was working with all kinds of dough and fillings late into the night. Lucky me. The cookies made with this recipe were the tastiest of the bunch and they happen to look exactly like the cookie emoji.

(VARIATIONS): We based this recipe on "1-2-3 cookies," where the proportions of sugar, butter and flour are 1-2-3 (by weight). If you maintain these proportions, you can certainly vary things. We've tried it by replacing part of the butter with tahini. You can also leave out the tahini and use 4½ tbsp (65 g) butter (the recipe uses a bit more tahini because there's less fat in it). Or replace the tahini with peanut butter, another nut butter or miso. In terms of add-ins, you can use any color of chocolate chip, nuts or sesame seeds. I always like bits of coarsely chopped chocolate: They will look less like the emoji cookies, though.

(LEFTOVERS): This recipe makes 2 big cookies or 4 small ones. You can eat them all in one sitting or gradually over a couple days. The dough will also keep in the fridge for at least 5 days. So you could bake half and make the rest a few days later when you want to have fresh cookies again.

3 tbsp + 1 tsp (50 g) butter, at room temperature
1 large tbsp (25 g) tahini
2½ tbsp (30 g) granulated sugar
Salt
¾ cup (100 g) all-purpose flour
⅓ cup (50 g) chocolate chips
Flaky sea salt

Preheat the oven to 340°F (170°C).

In a bowl, combine the butter, tahini, sugar and a pinch of salt using a wooden spoon. You can also grate the butter if it's straight from the fridge, which makes it easier to mix. Add the flour and most of the chocolate chips (but save some for decorating). Stir just until the dough comes together. Overmixing will make the cookies tough.

Make 2 or 4 balls out of the dough, flatten them into cookies and place on a baking sheet, spacing them apart. They won't expand in the oven, so just make them the size you want, ensuring they're about ¼ inch (0.5 cm) thick. Press a few more chocolate chips into the dough. Bake for 10 minutes. The inside may still be pale, but the outside should have browned edges. Remove the cookies from the oven and sprinkle with flaky sea salt. Let cool briefly, then devour.

Acknowledgments

As always, but more so this year, thanks to my dearest, most fantastic publisher, Miriam. I'm really looking forward to making our next book together and dancing at the book ball. I also want to thank: Sophia, for helping me research everything and for the most beautiful photos yet again; Marieke and Niqué, for helping me find a path forward whenever I got stuck; Jelle, for a design more incredible and beautiful than I ever could have imagined; Wouter, for everything; Yvette and Oof, for letting me borrow flatware; Sanne Fleur, Dad, Grandpa, Grandma and neighbor Steffie, for making my solo palace even better. Thank you, of course, to the recipe testers: Lizzy, Partoe, Sanne, Gijsje, Joyce and Alexandra. Without you, the recipes would have been quite a bit less readable.

Solo

English translation copyright © 2025 Robert Rose Inc.

Published originally in Dutch under the title Solo © 2024 by Nijgh Cuisine, Amsterdam

Text copyright © 2024 Emma de Thouars

Photographs copyright © Sophia van den Hoek, Studio Unfolded

Cover & text design copyright © 2024 Nijgh Cuisine, Amsterdam

No part of this publication may be reproduced, stored in a retrieval system or transmitted, in any form or by any means, without the prior written consent of the publisher or a licence from the Canadian Copyright Licensing Agency (Access Copyright). For an Access Copyright licence, visit www.accesscopyright.ca or call toll-free: 1-800-893-5777.

Library and Archives Canada Cataloguing in Publication

Title: Solo : embrace the pleasure of cooking for yourself / Emma de Thouars.

Other titles: Solo. English

Names: Thouars, Emma de, author.

Description: Includes index. | Translation of: Solo: recepten en tips voor als je het rijk alleen heb.

Identifiers: Canadiana 20250167557 | ISBN 9780778807360 (hardcover)

Subjects: LCSH: Cooking for one. | LCGFT: Cookbooks.

Classification: LCC TX652 .T4813 2025 | DDC 641.5/611—dc23

Translator: Lawrence Koch

Food Styling: Emma de Thouars

Food Photography & Styling: Sophia van den Hoek, Studio Unfolded

Editors: Julia Hulleman & Meredith Dees

Technical Editor: Jennifer MacKenzie

Cover & Design: Jelle F. Post

Layout & Production (English): PageWave Graphics Inc.

We acknowledge the support of the Government of Canada.

Canadä

Published by Robert Rose Inc.

120 Eglinton Avenue East, Suite 800, Toronto, Ontario, Canada M4P 1E2

Tel: (416) 322-6552 Fax: (416) 322-6936

www.robertrose.ca

Printed and bound in China

1 2 3 4 5 6 7 8 9   ESP   33 32 31 30 29 28 27 26 25